Opening a Restaurant or Other Food Business Starter Kit

How to Prepare a Restaurant Business Plan & Feasibility Study

With Companion CD-ROM

Sharon Fullen

**Opening a Restaurant or Other Food Business Starter Kit:
How to Prepare a Restaurant Business Plan & Feasibility
Study—With Companion CD-ROM**

Atlantic Publishing Group, Inc. Copyright © 2005
1210 SW 23rd Place • Ocala, Florida 34474
800-541-1336 • 352-622-5836–Fax
www.atlantic-pub.com
sales@atlantic-pub.com

SAN Number :268-1250

International Standard Book Number: 0-910627-36-3

Library of Congress Cataloging-in-Publication Data

Fullen, Sharon L.
Opening a restaurant or other food business starter kit : how to prepare a restaurant business plan & feasibility study : with companion
cd-rom / by Sharon Fullen.
     p. cm.
  Includes index.
  ISBN 0-910627-36-3 (alk. paper)
1. Restaurant management.
2. New business enterprises--Management.
3. Small business--Management. I. Title.

TX911.3.M27F835 2004
647.95'068--dc22

                                   2004022739

            10 9 8 7 6 5 4 3 2 1

Table of Contents

Chapter 3
Hiring a Business Plan Writer

Chapter 4
Business Plan Software

Chapter 5
What Does a Good Business Plan Contain?

Chapter 6
Writing a Feasibility Analysis

Chapter 7
Your Marketing Plan

Chapter 8
Financial Data

Chapter 9
Researching Your Business Concept

Chapter 10
Writing Your Plan

Chapter 11
Getting Your Plan "Published"

Chapter 12
Mini Strategic Plans

Chapter 13
Revising and Updating Your Business Plan

Chapter 14
Business Plan Writing Resources

Chapter 15
Sample Business Plan

Introduction

Starting your own restaurant is an exciting adventure. Close your eyes and visualize how the dining room looks, lust for the latest cooking equipment, smell your signature dish and see the faces of happy customers. Now think about writing a business plan for your new restaurant. Jars your eyes open and makes you sweat, doesn't it? Take a deep breath, help is on the way. *Opening a Restaurant or Other Food Business Starter Kit: How to Prepare a Restaurant Business Plan & Feasibility Study* was written to give first-time entrepreneurs and seasoned restaurateurs the support and guidance they need to make their dreams a reality.

You've taken a big first step by purchasing this book. Perhaps your banker or lender has told you that he MUST have a copy of your business plan or a friend suggested that you write a business plan. At this point, you may not actually know why you should bother. Just like writing a school paper, you probably are approaching this reluctantly. There are businesses that become successful without a business plan—but significantly more fail to plan and then fail to succeed.

There is no magic wand you can wave to speed you through the tough aspects of launching and operating a food service establishment, but with good planning, you can minimize the pain and maximize the benefits. The goal of this book is to help you P.L.A.N.:

Prepare for Success
Learn How to Be Profitable
Act, Not React
Navigate Pitfalls

Your Elevator Pitch

Your elevator pitch, which should take about the length of an elevator ride to deliver, is a brief description that neatly sums up your business concept. It isn't just a lifeless declaration—"I want to start a Chinese restaurant"; it is a statement that captures the excitement and potential of your idea—"I'm starting a trendy restaurant featuring exquisite dinners from every region of China. I've hired a chef from a trendy New York establishment and renowned restaurant designer Barbara Lazaroff is working with us."

Imagine you were alone in an elevator with billionaire Donald Trump. Here is your chance to pitch your idea to him. Can you capture his attention, sell him on your idea and intrigue his entrepreneurial spirit before you reach the 22nd floor?

Your elevator pitch is also a useful tool that helps you focus on your goals. You'll find several ways to build upon your elevator pitch throughout the book. Now set aside some quiet time with a pad and paper (or make your notes right on these pages), and start the process of creating your own plan for success.

1

What Is a Business Plan?

As you begin exploring the possibilities of opening a new restaurant or enhancing your current business, many ideas, emotions and dreams are bouncing around in your head. Should you do this or would that be better? So many things to think about, where do you start? The answers are within the entrepreneur's best guide and decision-making tool — your business plan!

I don't know too many people who are excited about the prospect of writing their business plan. It requires you to do extensive research, ask many questions, calculate current and future financial pictures and do some real soul searching. Nevertheless, the benefits are worth the effort. Once you get everything down on paper, I'm confident you'll be glad you invested the time to think through the "good, bad and the ugly" so that you can be prepared to handle a multitude of business situations. If your personal future and business success isn't worth the time and effort it takes to write your business plan — then perhaps you should rethink whether you are ready to be a restaurant owner.

A business plan is a document where you:

1. Describe your new or existing business.

2. Define your customers' needs and your ability to meet them.

3. Explore competitor strengths and weaknesses to outperform them.

4. Address possible stumbling blocks to success.

5. Establish yourself and your team as capable businesspeople and food artists.

6. Detail marketing strategies to capture your share of the market.

7. Set benchmarks and goals for launching, developing and profit making.

8. Provide financial projections and returns on investment.

9. Ask for money to support your success.

10. Tell investors and lenders what's in it for them.

In the following chapters, you'll learn how to develop a plan that addresses all ten of these purposes.

Still panicked about writing a business plan? Remember that your plan is a collection of information and ideas based upon your knowledge, expertise, background and faith **at that time.** Your plan isn't a rigid set of rules to live by, but a powerful living guide. As you move through each stage of your business development, you'll learn new facts and gain additional experience that may alter your path and goals.

Why Do I Need a Plan?

You need a Business Plan to explore your business ideas, determine their viability and secure money to make your ideas happen. Most people concentrate on the last reason—to get money. Their plan is then written solely to attract outside investors or satisfy lender requirements. If you are writing your plan primarily for them, you are at risk of slanting the truth and overlooking other areas that will benefit **you.**

How You Can Benefit

Researching and writing your business plan offers multiple benefits for new and experienced restaurant owners. The process of developing the plan helps you solidify your desires and set your professional goals. Writing your plan will:

1. **Clarify your vision.** Instead of just saying, "I'd like to own a restaurant," you'll be creating a Technicolor version of your cozy little Italian deli or your sleek and sophisticated restaurant featuring live jazz.

2. **Prove your potential.** You'll prove to yourself and

others that your community needs another steakhouse or tearoom. On the other hand, you may even discover that your idea isn't a viable one. Too much competition, wrong location, inadequate customer base or insufficient customer demand are all reasons to stop and reassess your ideas.

3. **Look at obstacles.** Every business venture will have obstacles. By looking at potential problems and outlining solutions, you'll prepare yourself. Not all problem/solution scenarios will make it into your plan, but you'll uncover many of them as you research your business prospects.

4. **Determine your business viability.** Are your goals achievable with the people, time and money resources you have available to you? Is the idea too trendy? Will it have sufficient lifespan to repay lenders? Will investors be attracted to the idea?

5. **Project your success.** Will your restaurant provide you with the personal and financial rewards you are seeking? Can you physically or emotionally deal with the workload? Do you have sufficient experience to make it happen?

6. **Secure ample capital.** By projecting your cash flow and working capital needs, you'll have a better understanding of how much money you will have coming through the door every day to pay your

vendors, lenders and employees. Before you invest your entire nest egg or borrow more money, you must decide if you'll have enough money (from every possible source) to keep you afloat until profits roll in. Insufficient capitalization is a primary reason new businesses fail.

Great Risks, Great Rewards

As an entrepreneur, you are the one with the greatest investment and the most at risk. Your financial future, emotional and physical health and reputation are on the line. Sure, investors and lenders have a risk—that's why they ask for ownership rights or charge interest. A well-researched business plan looks at and analyzes various risk factors. No one likes to think about failing, but truthfully, the success rate for new restaurants is not exceptionally high. The better prepared you are, the more likely you will be one of the successful ones.

Everyone focuses on the process of writing the plan. How do I convince the lender to grant the loan? What if my writing skills aren't the best? We'll address these issues in later chapters. Right now, I want you to concentrate on research. Corporations invest millions on research before launching a new sales division or product line. Your diligence in researching your customer demographics, competitors, equipment purchases, menu choices and more is just as important. It is your key to determining whether your dream can be successful.

No Profits, No Reason

Sometimes business owners discover after months of research and number crunching that their idea has insufficient profit potential. As you look at all the variables, create sales and expense reports and set budgets, you must be proving that you will be profitable within a reasonable time. These profit points also must be worth your time and effort. It isn't just earning money that counts, but is it enough to finance your growth, pay your employees fairly, provide a quality product and have enough to live on?

However, if your plan tells you that your idea isn't a profit-maker, it will have been time well spent. Saving yourself from potential financial ruin, long-term debt and stress is an invaluable lesson.

Who Should Review Your Business Plan

Your business plan should be reviewed by your accountant and legal counsel (who should have been consulted on specific sections of the plan). Their comments (even outside of their expertise) can be invaluable for catching confusing passages or fine-tuning ideas.

Your banker would be the next person who might assist you. In some smaller communities, businesspeople will have a personal relationship with a local bank. Even if you are not seeking a loan, a business specialist banker has experience in reviewing business plans and can give you feedback.

Other Outside Advisors and Consultants

You may find other people in your community who can provide you with advice, recommendations and a critique of your plan. Your local university or community college may have a business development advisor on staff. SCORE, a volunteer program manned by retired businesspeople, provides no- or low-cost counseling aimed at helping businesspeople succeed. You can find more information on SCORE at **www.score.org.** You'll find additional advisory resources throughout the book and in *Chapter 14 — Resources.*

Who Will Use Your Business Plan

Investors (family, friends, outside professionals) will need a full version of your business plan to review its profitability potential. Lenders (bank, credit union, government, family/ friends) will also need a full version to determine your ability to repay loans. Both will be looking at your idea along with your financial projections.

Your insurance agent may want to see sections of your plan to help them determine your business insurance needs such as liability, auto, fire, casualty, theft and life.

Your real estate broker may want to see sections of your plan to help you locate the right property (land or land and building) for your new restaurant. Your architect, builder/contractor may also want to review parts of your plan as they begin designing a new building, planning renovations or specifying remodeling projects. Other designers (landscape, interior, kitchen, lighting, sound) may also benefit from seeing your vision.

Confidentiality/Non-Disclosure Agreements

The information you gather and report in your business plan is confidential. While it may not be top secret, it may be in your best interest to have interested parties sign a non-disclosure agreement before receiving your plan to read. A non-disclosure agreement outlines that the information is proprietary and confidential and not to be shared, copied, distributed or discussed with unauthorized parties. This agreement can be verbal or written. Should a violation of the agreement occur, a written agreement is your best bet. Investors may be hesitant to sign a non-disclosure agreement; however, terms can be negotiated. Your attorney can assist you with an appropriate agreement for your situation and advise you on when to use it.

Please note: Bankers, lenders and venture capitalists are professionals bound to confidentiality. Requiring a non-disclosure agreement (and/or contract clause) may be considered insulting; so be careful when requiring a signed agreement.

What Interested Parties Should Find in Your Plan

Everyone who reads your business plan will be looking for something different based upon his or her needs. The messages within your plan can play an important roll in selling your concept; these are the soul of your business and can affect how people respond to your requests for support. Even bankers, who want to see strong financials, are looking for a gut reaction that tells them you are worth the investment.

Your Family

Your first support group should be your family members. Your spouse and children are your most important allies. Your husband/wife and older children may also be your business partners. Even if this isn't a family business, it will put additional demands on everyone, require you to be working long hours, distract you from family activities, and create stress. Enlist your extended family in your vision and let them read your plan. You'll have a network of people interested in your success (however, beware that this may color their opinions and mean you aren't hearing the truth). In addition, family members are a common source of start-up capital.

> *Your family should see why your dream is important to you and how they can take an active role in its success.*

Your Partners

Whether you have a silent or active partnership arrangement, everyone should share the vision expressed in the plan. You won't be detailing assigned duties but general responsibilities based upon experience and skills will be outlined. If you have partners, you'll be writing the plan together. You may co-author each section or only work on specific sections that require your expertise. If partners are assigned sections to research and write, be certain that the writing style and "voice" remain consistent throughout to avoid confusing the reader.

> *Partner(s) should see a healthy partnership, a mutual respect and their value to the business in your restaurant's business plan.*

Your Lender

Anyone who gives you money in exchange for periodic payments and interest is a lender. Lenders can be a family member or friend, a bank, private organization or a government agency.

- **Family members and friends.** Borrowing from family members and friends can be an excellent way to finance your business launch or growth. While you may not have a lengthy loan application, you should treat these loans just as seriously as you would a bank loan. Have your attorney draw up an appropriate contract for all parties to sign.

Creating a financial relationship with family and friends can have more than financial risks. Everyone must separate the business arrangement from personal interactions. You should also consider what might happen if you are unable to repay the loan according to its terms or should your business fail. Even if everyone shakes hands and agrees to the lender/borrower terms, people just cannot seem to separate their personal feelings when it comes to doing business with family and friends.

Private lenders should be able to see that they are making a loan that can be repaid. They'll probably think of it more like an investment in your future.

- **Bankers.** Your banker may be an advocate for your business. Additional business banking services may also be available to you just for the asking. In the age of ATMs and Web-based banks, many of us have lost touch with the value of a bank professional. However, even major national bank conglomerates often offer business (and even small business) services through a specific department. Regional and state banks often use their individualized business banking services as a way to set themselves apart from the national banks. Shop around for a small-business banker and meet him or her face to face.

This relationship can prove to be invaluable and costs you nothing more than your time. Secured loans use real property (business or personally owned) or other tangible assets as collateral. However, there are other types of collateral such as community economic development, personal goodwill or just your potential for success.

Bankers should see that your business will have ample capital and resources (people and things) for continual operation over several months (and maybe even more than a year) and sufficient profits to pay back your loan on time.

- **Private organizations.** Depending upon your community's economic needs, you may qualify for financial support in the way of low-interest loans or grants (essentially a financial gift) through privately funded organizations and associations. These funds are typically used to stimulate economic development in high-risk communities or economic parity for woman and minorities. Check your local business development agency to see if they have a list of private loans and grant programs.

  Philanthropic organizations should see that you, your community and your restaurant meet their criteria for economic support. They will consider your ability to repay your loan. If you are applying for a grant, they will look at your potential for success, contribution to the community (creating jobs, paying taxes, rejuvenating neighborhoods) and need.

21

- **Government agencies.** Have you ever seen the guy in the loud suit with question marks shouting on TV about the millions to be had from government agencies for whatever purposes you can dream up? The fact is there actually are national, state and county agencies that can provide you with loans and grants.

  The federal government, through the Small Business Administration, is a major supporter of small businesses. The SBA doesn't directly loan you money, as their role is to underwrite small business loans through local banks. You'll need to meet all SBA loan requirements along with the bank's.

  Publicly funded grants operate similarly to privately funded ones and are targeted at people and communities that need economic stimulus.

  Government agencies should see that your business would be capable of repaying loans. Grant applications will be reviewed for their ability to satisfy the grant program's mission.

Your Investors

Any person or business who gives you money in exchange for a share of ownership is an investor. Investors can be a family member or friend, an angel investor or a venture capitalist.

Investors typically come into play when you are unable to obtain a conventional loan. Where as a lender might be charging 9.5 percent interest and has no stake in your business, investors will want to own a percentage of your restaurant. Ownership equals a greater risk, so this money will cost you more. You'll not only have a financial relationship, you may also be entering into a partnership. While your investor(s) may not actually help you run your restaurant, they will have expectations and needs that you'll have to meet.

Investors should see that your business has an excellent profit potential. They'll be looking at your numbers first. A plan that doesn't demonstrate an ample return on their investment may not be worth their time. They'll also want to see that you and your team have the ability to start and operate a successful restaurant.

Your Partners

Your partners may be active participants in your daily operations or silent partners that work behind the scenes in financial and legal issues. Investors owning a share of your business are also like silent partners. Typically, you and your partners would develop your business plan together; however, you may write your plan to help you secure one. Perhaps you are a talented chef looking for a partner with more front-of-the-house experience or you are a great restaurant manager and searching for a partner with outstanding culinary talents.

Your partners should to see that their contributions are valued. Their role in the business should provide them with more than money — it should fulfill their entrepreneurial dreams also.

Your Employees

Key personnel such as head chefs, master bakers and managers not only serve your customers, they also serve you. Their energy, enthusiasm, expertise and input are the foundation of your business. If you have an existing business, involve your staff in the development or update of your business plan. You may not feel comfortable sharing specific aspects of your financial plan; however, involving your staff in researching, developing and writing portions of the plan can be a wise decision. Not only can you tap into their skills and expertise, you also empower them to think creatively and to own the idea. This ownership mentality is invaluable in making your goals and creating a successful restaurant.

> *Your employees should see how they can make a difference, what your mutual goals are, and how you will actively support them. Your plan can also establish success benchmarks, business guidelines and employee performance standards.*

Your Suppliers

As a new business, establishing yourself with vendors can be arduous. Even existing businesses often have failed to develop strong business partnerships with their suppliers only to discover that there is little or no goodwill to trade upon. You may find it advantageous to share sections of your business plan with select vendors. While companies don't base your established credit line on projections and owner bios, you may find partners who will extend you courtesies and considerations that you hadn't even considered. Solid companies want to build long-term relationships with trusted customers. Sharing your vision and potential may be a way to start that relationship.

> *Your suppliers should see the fiscal wisdom of your endeavor and see the payoff (in long-term business with increasing purchase volume). Select vendors may learn how you intend to use equipment/services and how their working with you can prove profitable for everyone.*

2

Who Should Write Your Business Plan?

As I've emphasized already, the person who gains the most wisdom from the research and writing of the business plan is you. By writing the plan yourself (or with the help of business partners or key employees), you will be able to document your ideas, ensure that the research is appropriate and accurate, and gain a better understanding of the financial aspects of operating your restaurant. Your business plan should incorporate your dreams and passions—no one else is better suited to that task.

But I Only Want to Be a Restaurateur

The analysis skills used in developing your business plan are the same one's you'll use to become a successful restaurant owner. There is no better time than now—before you become consumed with daily business needs—to learn all about your community and competitors, practice reading and interpreting financial reports, calculate your break-even numbers, and create a real-world, I-can-be-successful-with-this budget. Once you aggressively begin your launch, you'll need to make quick decisions based upon solid research. When your doors open, having this information gives you a solid foundation to successfully handle the difficulties that are inevitable in any business.

If you are hesitant about your own research and writing skills, there are plenty of resources to guide you, along with experts to review and fine-tune your finished plan. There are books, software programs, support consultants, classes and seminars designed to help you with the gathering and writing process. When I say "do-it-yourself," I am referring to you being the primary developer of your business plan, but that doesn't mean outside support isn't encouraged. Remember, you're already getting outside expert advice as you read this book!

If after reading this book you still feel uncertain about writing your own business plan, there are other sources for business plan advice and training.

Web-Based Advice

The Web is brimming with information on writing business plans. In fact, you can become overwhelmed with all the free advice online. To make it easier, I have created a list of some of the best sites (*Chapter 14 – Resources*).

Business Plan Classes

You can take classes or attend seminars online, via the telephone, at your local community college or through your state's small-business or economic development agency.

Local business plan writing classes for entrepreneurs are an excellent time and money investment. You'll not only learn the standard format (what your plan **must** address), you'll be taught plenty of other skills that you'll find helpful as a restaurant owner. You'll have peers to network with and classes often feature local experts (bankers, accountants, lawyers, etc.) who also offer one-on-one counseling.

Local Classes

You will find business plan writing classes and seminars by contacting:

- SCORE (**www.score.org**) for local classes.

- NxLevel (**www.nxlevel.org**) for local nonprofit programs and classes.

- Your community college or university's school of business.

- Your city's chamber of commerce or state's small-business development agency.

- Local economic development nonprofit organizations.

- Your business banker or accountant.

- Your state and/or national restaurant and food service associations. (*Chapter 14 – Resources* lists many national associations and trade organizations).

- Local newspapers (and their Web sites) and business journals.

Online Classes

You can attend a class at your convenience on the Web. Here are a few available sources:

- Writing Trainers (**www.writingtrainers.com**)

- Web Campus (**www.webcampus.stevens.edu**)

- Small Biz Lending and SBA (**www.smallbizlending.com/resources/workshop/sba.htm**) slideshow class.

Teleclasses

A teleclass is where you call a specific phone number and punch in an assigned code. You are then connected with the lecturer and other attendees. Typically, you'll have to pay any long-distance fees in addition to the tuition. Here are a few available sources.

- Rebel Business (**www.rebelbusiness.com**)

- Career Masters Institute (**www.cminstitute.com /EntreprenurialEagles.html**) — a variety of business teleclasses

- Parker Associates (**www.asparker.com /freecoaching.html**) — free teleclass

- Write Your Own Pink Slip
  (**www.writeyourownpinkslip.com**) — teleclasses

Seminar Workshops

- Quantum Business Solutions (**www.qbizsolutions
  .net**) — touring workshops.

- Score (**www.score56.org/seminars_workshops.html**) —
  list of local seminars.

Software-Specific Classes

When reviewing and choosing business plan software, check out
online tutorials and/or third-party consultants to guide you with
specific business plan software packages. These classes should
not be for software technical support, but how to write your plan
using the tools provided.

Books

Besides all of the valuable information provided here, there are
other books that you might find helpful. You'll find resource
books listed in *Chapter 14 — Resources* and by topic throughout
this book.

Software Programs

There are several business plan software programs designed to
help you gather your thoughts and write a standardized plan for
restaurant operators. Others will provide you with text ideas and
a boilerplate format. Beware that cutting and pasting canned text
will result in an ordinary plan with little individuality. To learn
more about several popular business plan-preparation software
packages, see *Chapter 4 — Business Plan Software*.

If you simply cannot see yourself writing your own business plan, there are business plan writers out there who, for a fee, will do all the dirty work.

3

Hiring a Business Plan Writer

If you simply cannot see yourself writing your own business plan, there are business plan writers out there who, for a fee, will do all the dirty work. As an experienced business plan writer, I personally understand why people come to me; however, I also know the value of writing your own plan as I've written plans for my own business ventures.

You might consider the services of a restaurant consultant for writing your plan and/or conducting a feasibility study to determine the potential for your business venture. For more information on Feasibility Studies, see Chapter 6.

Here's what you should look for in a business plan writer.

A well-qualified business plan writer will have:

1. **Writing experience.** Review sample business plans, along with other business writing. It takes a specific talent to be able to write insightful and compelling business documents. Remember, your plan is 1) a sales

piece to sell your idea, 2) a plan of action, and 3) a set of realistic and attainable goals.

2. **Research experience.** Unlike writing a work of fiction, you'll need facts and analysis to support your ideas. Can your business plan writer handle a portion of this for you? Does he or she know what types of research are needed to create a customized plan?

3. **Listening abilities.** Your plan is a reflection of your dreams and desires. Never hire someone who doesn't listen carefully to what you have to say.

4. **Questions.** Does he or she ask lots of in-depth questions or just want you to fill out a short form to work from? The more he or she knows about you, your business proposal and your concept, the better your finished plan will be.

5. **A business background.** Does he or she have a business background that will give an understanding of what it takes to be a successful businessperson? Business training can be a plus.

6. **Strong references.** Word-of-mouth is the best way to find any service provider. Ask other businesspeople for a referral. If that isn't possible, ask for a list of references that you can contact personally.

What It Will Cost You

Paying for a comprehensive plan can be costly with pricing based upon the research required, length of plan, turnaround time and financial reports to be generated. There is no typical plan fee because a custom plan will have a custom price. You can expect to pay $1,200 to $10,000 for a top-notch professional business plan. Pricing variables are also based on your intended use, local prevailing rates and the expertise of the plan writer.

You must be aware that it takes time to develop a professional business plan and time is money; $150–$300 plans will be boilerplate projects that cover just the basics. Outside investors and lenders see these often and won't give you any bonus points for this type of professionally written plan. Be aware that your pay-and-go plan may be a poor investment.

Above the basic plan level, you will receive more personalized service and some advice. Review what is included with any quote along with any built-in review and revision procedures. Once you sign off and accept your plan, additional work will mean additional costs.

You'll be required to pay a deposit, periodic payments (for projects running more than a month) and the balance upon completion.

Searching for a Business Plan Writer

Before you begin the search process, you need to be able to tell potential candidates what you want, when you want it and what data and information you can give them to work with. Writers may actually interview you. Others will have complex forms that you'll complete. The better prepared you are, the better results you'll get.

Tell Them What You Need

When interviewing potential business plan writers (also known as business plan consultants), the first thing you should do is clarify who does what. Will you have to provide them with all background research on customers, competitors, economic situations and financial reports? Can the consultant provide you with secondary research (see *Chapter 8 – Researching Your Plan*)? If the writer isn't local, who will gather community-specific information? Does the writer have restaurant plan experience? You'll save yourself time and money if you do some basic research (for example, read this entire book) on what you need in and from your business plan.

Tell Them What You Want

Write down some specifics. Create a list of purposes and who will be reviewing your finished plan. Develop your elevator speech describing your future or current business (see *Introduction* on writing your elevator pitch). Don't be afraid to share your passion; if you bore your prospective plan writers with the facts, they may never catch the spirit. A business plan is a business document but it is also a sales piece – you'll be selling investors, lenders and others on your concept and ability to be profitable.

Your goal is to be able to say to prospective business plan writers "I need…" Even if your chosen plan-writing expert directs you differently, you'll have a place to start the exploration.

Tell Them When You Need It

Writers will need to have an approximate completion date to provide you with a quote. If your time frame is flexible, you won't be paying any rush charges. However, don't let it drag on or you'll lose your momentum and frustrate your consultant.

Tell Them What Resources You Have

Will you be providing all the supporting data? Do you have research that you have already completed? Do you have an accountant who will help with the financials? Is there an attorney to advise and review your business structure? Do you have a business plan that you have used in the past? What else can you provide the writer so they can deliver what you want and need?

Write an RFP

In choosing a business plan writer, you must be able to tell each prospective consultant your requirements. The more specific you can be, the more accurate the quotes will be. A good way to accomplish that is with a written Request for Proposal (also known as an RFP).

An RFP describes the task (service/product) to be provided, outlines the scope of the need, establishes what qualifications are required, and asks consultants to bid. Having a set of rules from which to work will help consultants give you an accurate quote. In addition, you'll know that each bid is based upon the same criteria so you don't have to factor in variables when comparing pricing and services to be provided.

If I Could Only Write an RFP

RFPs can be quite report-like; however, a basic outline clearly defining your needs and expectations can be quite adequate for quoting purposes. Quotes will be based upon your specifications so provide as much information as possible, be accurate and have a clear set of expectations. You'll need a brief RFP if you want to search for business plan writers through various consultant and business service Web sites such as Guru (**www.guru.com**) or eLance (**www.elance.com**). Many of these sites are free to businesses seeking assistance.

Contracts and Agreements

Your business plan writer should have a standard consulting contract that you will read carefully and sign. This should be reviewed by your attorney prior to signing. The contract should be a work-for-hire agreement where you own all copyrights to the complete plan including all original research, artwork, diagrams and charts. The contract should also prevent the writer from using your name or any part of your plan for advertising or marketing purposes without your written permission. You may also want to include a non-disclosure agreement.

The contract will also outline periodic payments and what constitutes completed and accepted. You'll want to watch for errors and omissions, and don't sign off on anything that isn't correct to the best of your knowledge. You will be accepting the plan as accurate and presenting the facts as true to investors and lenders.

Confidentiality/Non-Disclosure Clauses

Again, you must remember that you may be sharing confidential ideas and information with a stranger. A confidentiality (also known as non-disclosure) clause can be especially important if you are hiring someone locally where there is a greater chance that competitive restaurateurs would use the same expert.

4

Business Plan Software

Technically all you need is a basic word processor, a calculator and a printer to turn out a professional-looking business plan. With this book and a few online reference sites, you may be able to write your own business plan from scratch. However, not everyone feels comfortable with the process and the financial data and projections typically trip up most new entrepreneurs. That's where business plan software can come to your rescue.

The interactive nature of business planning software can help you through the entire process and make it a very wise investment. Software templates with a fill-in-the-blanks format and sample business plans can stimulate ideas and help you get over a frightening blank page. Most commercial products offer sample plans for restaurants and other food service businesses. A few have specific tools for launching a new restaurant or for seeking improvement capital for existing restaurants.

This chapter will talk about these various software packages and their related cousins, Web-based business plan development services. I'll also give you some tips on using software you may already own to create a professional-looking finished plan.

Too Good to Be True

No matter what any of the software packages or Web programs promise:

- You cannot write a solid, well-researched business plan in a day.

- You may not get financing, even if they guarantee it!

- You will need some basic knowledge of accounting practices and financial reporting, just as you will need these to be a successful restaurateur.

- You should never use the canned text provided. Review the examples and use your own words based upon your own beliefs and research. The provided text typically isn't outstanding and the writing is often recognizable to seasoned lenders and investors.

Try Before You Buy

With Internet access, you can view demos online and download trial versions. Most trial versions have all the features available to test except saving and printing. Some software developers offer food service, restaurant and hospitality templates and sample plans. Review these for appropriateness. However, software that is not industry-specific can be just as helpful combined with this book.

Your Software Choices

Accounting Software

QuickBooks Premiere 2003 and up (Intuit®, **www.quickbooks .intuit.com**) has built in financial planning capabilities including a Business Planner function using Ultimate Business Planner (see following information). If you have not purchased an accounting package, choosing the Premiere version (over the Pro version) of QuickBooks gives you the $99 business plan package.

Intuit's Quicken Home and Business versions offer some limited financial projection capabilities. Their business planning interactive link refers you to Palo Alto Software, makers of Business Plan Pro (see following information). Microsoft Money Small Business Edition also has some basic financial planning capabilities.

Word Processing Software

Word processors offer outline capabilities and other document writing features. Business plan templates are available free from Microsoft at **http://office.microsoft.com/templates**. If you are an experienced word processor and spreadsheet user, you may find that these two are all you need. If you own WordPerfect or another full-featured word processor, check the template folder and their Web site for additional resources.

Spreadsheet Software

Excel (part of the Microsoft Office Suite) and other spreadsheet programs now come with a variety of financial and accounting templates. Additional templates such as break-even analysis and start-up costs for Microsoft products are available at the address listed above. Lotus 1-2-3 and other full-featured spreadsheets offer similar sales projection and financial-reporting templates.

Presentation Software

You may want to include an electronic presentation and/or graphics in your business plan. PowerPoint (found in the Microsoft Office Suite) can be a useful tool. Free templates can be found on the same Microsoft address.

More Free Templates

Below are a few resources for free business plan templates. Remember the adage; you get what you pay for. All work with the Microsoft Office line.

1. Bank of Canada (**http://www.bdc.ca/en /business_tools/business_plan**)—free English and French versions

2. VFinance (**www.vfinance.com**)—free downloadable template

3. Free Webs (**www.freewebs.com/business_plans**)

4. VCAonline (**www.vcaonline.com/resources /bizplan/freetemplate.asp**)

5. SCORE (**www.score.org/template_gallery.html**)—free templates

Later in this chapter, I'll discuss template-based business plan software that can be purchased.

Business Plan-Specific Software

There are two basic versions of business planning software: stand-alone and template-based. Stand-alone software is a complete package and only requires a computer and printer. Template-based (also known as add-on software) are forms and guides to be viewed and used within common word processing and spreadsheet programs.

- **Which should I choose?** The answer is the one you believe you'll feel most comfortable using. Why struggle with learning something new and potential technical issues when the purpose is to make your plan development easier? However, you'll have more choices if you select a stand-alone version.

- **Should I spend more on software to get a better plan?** Spending more isn't necessary as the true value of your plan is what **you** put into it. The professional packages available from leading software manufactures are developed by marketing and executive experts. Just like this book, these software packages are lifeless guides until you put your personality and enthusiasm into them. The software itself is not typically the critical part of the package; although, there may be features such as importing Excel spreadsheet data that make using it easier. It is the guidance and advice that goes with it that establishes its overall value.

- **I need help with my financial section.** Some packages provide extensive financial-reporting capabilities. Food service-specific financial formulas and ratios are available on some packages. Preformatted spreadsheet or financial calculators will increase the cost of the software package, but if you will be handling the projections by yourself, the investment is worth it.

One of the best ways of selecting a business plan software package is a personal recommendation. Ask your family, friends and other business owners (don't forget your accountant) for their experiences. Even if you get an old review, significant software changes or enhancements are rare except for Web-based plan writing and the support resources available on the manufacturer's Web site.

Popular Business Plan Packages

Stand-Alone Products

Business Plan Pro (Palo Alto Software, **www.paloalto.com**), introduced in 1995, is a top seller (at press time ranks 127 in sales at Amazon.com). This package has a standard addition retailing at $99 and a premier edition at $199. The premier edition allows you to collaborate with others and offers additional financial spreadsheets and analysis tools. There are dozens of hospitality and food service industry sample plans for you to review.

Notes: Offers restaurant-specific support. An online Flash demo (requires Macromedia's Flash Web browser plug-in) is available online, along with a few sample restaurant plans. No downloadable trial version available. Works with Windows 98 and up, and requires 100MB of hard disk space. No Mac version. Requires Internet access for some features. Can import Intuit QuickBooks and Microsoft Excel data; however, does not require either program. Must cut-and-paste to insert word processing text. Available in English, Spanish and Portuguese and for United Kingdom and Canadian users. Up to four free technical support incidents (toll call, fax, e-mail) and $10 per call thereafter. Available at company site, office supply and software retailers, and major online bookstores.

Business Plan Writer Deluxe (Nova Development, **www.novadevelopment.com**) is priced competitively with Business Plan Pro's standard edition. A free trial can be downloaded from their site after providing them with basic contact information. A PlanAudit™ feature checks your plan for spelling, accuracy and math errors. Audio and video help is available, along with sample plans and case studies. This software provides forecasting and financial reporting with color charts. A 10,000-piece collection of business graphic clipart is included; however, this isn't typically of any significant value. Kiplinger's Business Attorney software with legal forms is included.

Notes: Requires Windows 98 and up. No Mac version. Can import QuickBooks® Pro data and export to Word and Excel. Can create PDF files. Multi-user collaboration requires Internet access and their Plan Write Central membership (no pricing shown on company Web site). Free technical support via e-mail or toll call. Available at company site, office supply and software retailers, and major online bookstores.

Ultimate Business Planner (Atlas Business Solutions, Inc., **www.bptools.com**) uses the question and answer format with explanations of terms.

> Notes: Powers QuickBooks Premier Business Planner; full version of this planner included in Intuit QuickBooks Premiere 2003 and up. Works with Windows 95 and up. No Mac version. Requires 16MB of hard disk space. Online demo slideshow. Ninety-day unconditional money-back guarantee. Thirty-day free technical support to toll number or via e-mail. Priced at $99 retail, it can be downloaded immediately from the company Web site or you can order a CD.

Plan Write (Business Resource Software, **www.brs-inc.com**) offers three versions of their plan software.

> **Plan Write for Loans** ($49.95) offers little customization, no sample business plans and two free technical support calls.

> **Plan Write for Business** ($119.95) is a full-fledged plan developer suitable for most business needs.

> **Plan Write Expert Edition** ($219.95) adds expert review and analysis of your finished plan. Their MBA Wizard™ is designed to learn and provide advice based upon your specific data. The Business and Expert editions come with unlimited free technical support.

Notes: Sixty-day money-back guarantee. Works with Windows 95 and up. No Mac version. Exports to Microsoft Word, Excel, HTML, PDF and Rich Text Format (.rft).

Template Products

Two important advantages for template-style business planning products are that they don't require you to learn anything new and they work with older Windows operating systems and Office packages.

PlanMagic Restaurant (PlanMagic, **www.planmagic.com**) are Microsoft Word and Excel templates. PlanMagic Restaurant offers an excellent selection of plan writing tools including a 125-page guide and 35 restaurant-specific Excel financial templates and PowerPoint presentation templates. Twelve months of free upgrades. For Windows 98 and above. Requires Internet access for download and Office 97 and above.

Business Plan Builder (Jian, **www.jian.com**) requires Microsoft Word and Excel as the basic components are templates and worksheets. Company touts they used software for a $210,000 SBA loan and $750,000 line of credit. Can forward plan through software to Kinko's for printing and binding. Sixty-day guarantee. Works with Windows 98 and up, Microsoft Office 97 and up. 24MB of hard disk space. Limited version available for Mac users—$20 less.

OfficeReady Business Plans (Template Zone, **www.templatezone.com/business-plan**) are templates for

Microsoft Office 97 and above. Templates are preformatted for Word, Excel and PowerPoint, with additional graphic support and advice. Works with Windows 95 and up.

Business Plan Template (Business Plan Success, **www.business-plan-success.com**). Again, these are templates that work for Microsoft Office 97 and above. Immediate download along with a variety of support guides. Works with Windows 95 and up.

For Mac Users

Mac users don't have much to choose from when it comes to programs written for the Apple operating system. Business Plan Builder offers a less expensive, scaled-down version for Mac users. (See prior paragraph for information.) A few manufacturers suggest using Microsoft's Virtual PC software to read Windows versions on your Mac. However, this is a costly solution; you are better off relying on your Mac word processor and spreadsheet. Any template that states that it will work with

Microsoft Word or Excel should work with Office for Mac. You can also use the free Microsoft templates mentioned earlier in this chapter.

Online Planning

Web-based business plan development services offer true fill-in-the-blank convenience and caveats. Via secure password-protected login, you would actually write your plan online. This may be a practical option when you need shared user access from a distance. However, writing online isn't as handy as it might seem. If you wander away, you may be logged out without saving your work. Don't forget to save your work-in-progress plan at every offered option.

You have a more limited ability to print and save online plans. Review site policies carefully including security and privacy policies. Many online business-planning services have a less than professional appearance and too low pricing to have the same value as the major software developers.

- The Entrepreneur's Center at (**www.thebeehive.org /ecenter/start/bizplan/business-plan-why.asp**) is one example of free online business planning.

- Budget 21 (**www.budget21.com**) offers a free trial to their online planning services and one-year access for $39.95.

- Planware (**www.planware.org/freeware.htm**) offers some free online strategic planning features.

- Fundable Plans (**www.fundableplans.com**) charges $39.95 to create your plan via the Web.

Check with your state's and the national food service/restaurant/hospitality associations for member discounts on planning software. Online food service industry forums can also be a great place for recommendations.

Still Don't Know What to Buy?

Find Accounting Software (**www.findaccountingsoftware.com**) is a free Web-based service that, based on a few classifying questions (including a 10–15 minute telephone interview), will help you select business management and planning software.

For a full review of several business plan software packages, visit Home Office Reports at **www.homeofficereports.com**.

5

What Does a Good Business Plan Contain?

Agood business plan contains dreams and ideas backed by facts and figures in a fairly standardized format. The standardized format makes it easier for lenders and investors (who look at hundreds and even thousands of business plans every month) to scan for specific information efficiently. Lenders may even just skim your plan and assign it to a lower level employee who will read it thoroughly

Investors, with more demanding criteria for funding, may not actually read your plan at all. They will be checking specific sections for the potential return on their investment. Your financial reports and projections will provide them with enough information to either reject your request, refer the plan to a subordinate for full follow-up, or read it in full.

Standard Business Plan Format

There are specific sections that must be included in your business plan; however, the format can be varied to explain your business thoroughly. You may find sample plans with different titles but the information will closely match the plan format outlined below.

Cover Page
Table of Contents

I.   Executive Summary

II.   Background Information

    a. Personal Information

        i. Personal Skills and Expertise

        ii. Personal Financial Capability

III. Business Concept

        i. Mission Statement

        ii. Business Goals and Objective

        iii. General Description of Business

IV.   Description of Products and Services

    a. Features of Products/Services

    b. Benefits to Customers

    c. Future Products/Services

V.   Management Structure and Organization

    a. Legal Form

    b. Ownership

    c. Management and Personnel

        iii. Capital Equipment and Supply List

    b. Income Projections (profit and loss statements)

        i. Three–Year Summary

        ii. Detail By Month, First Year

        iii. Detail By Quarters, Second and Third Years

        iv. Assumptions Upon Which Projections Are Based

    c. Cash Flow Projections

        i. Sales and Expenses Estimates

        ii. Monthly Cash Flow Projections

    d. Summary of Financial Needs

VIII. Conclusion

    a. Feasibility Statement

IX.   Support Documents

    a. Copies of Personal Financial Documents

    b. Copies of Franchise Contracts

    c. Copies of Lease Agreements

    d. Copies of Licenses

    e. Copies of Legal Documents

    f. Copy of Resumés

    g. Copies of Letters of Intent

Your plan will require some research to prove that your new restaurant concept or expansion has merit. *Chapter 7 – Financial Data* will discuss the financial data you'll need to present your business concept as a profitable one.

You might want to get out a pad and pen to jot down notes on how you'll complete each of the plan sections. Following the plan outline, I'll define unfamiliar terms and provide you with some thought-provoking ideas to explore that need to be conveyed section-by-section.

Cover Page

You'll need to include your legal business name, assumed business name (also known as "doing business as" or "DBA"), owner name(s), contact address, phone, fax and e-mail information.

Table of Contents

The last page you will write for your plan. *Chapter 9 – Writing Your Plan* talks about this process.

Executive Summary

Your executive summary is an abbreviated version of your entire plan, written to catch the attention of your most important audience. Often busy lenders or investors won't read beyond the executive summary and your financial projections; therefore, it is imperative that your executive summary is a strong distillation of your research and plans for success. You'll write this critical section **after** you've completed your plan.

Background Information

Personal Resources

The background section covers the personal assets — skills, expertise, financial and other personal resources — that all owners bring to the table. Like a resumé that gets you a dream job, this section will help you secure your dream business. The first half of this section should detail the work history, education, skills and talents that you and your partners will rely on to become successful restaurant owners. Outline the food service-specific creative talents and work experience of each owner.

This information is presented to assure lenders and investors that you have what it takes to manage your restaurant and deliver profits. If the food service experience of your ownership team is not exceptionally strong, emphasize your accumulated business skills. You will have an opportunity in subsequent sections to discuss the talent and expertise you will be hiring to fill any gaps in your background.

Financial Resources

Your financial resources will be of great consideration to lenders and investors. Start by creating a personal financial statement listing your assets and liabilities to determine your net worth. Your net worth (and especially assets that can be easily converted to cash) will be of great interest to franchisers, as many have minimum net worth requirements. Bankers want to know what you will require as earnings from your business. Insufficient business (or other financial resources) earnings can undermine your ability to repay loans or become profitable.

Your financial contributions to launching a new business or expanding a current one are also of great interest. Ideas without personal funding are considered high-risk investments. Remember that finding money to fund 100 percent of your dream is virtually impossible. Lenders and investors won't be interested in a plan that requires their funds be the only money at risk. As a new entrepreneur with no business assets, you will be asked to use your personal assets as loan collateral.

If you are turned down for outside funding because of a lack of personal finances, take your plan and transform it into a goal for yourself. Determine the percent of start-up and operating expenses you'll need to have in hand before you can present your plan again to investors and lenders.

Business Concept

Mission Statement

Also known as a statement of purpose, your mission statement is similar to the objective section of a resumé. This statement should capture the reasons why you personally want to be in business, what you want to accomplish with your business, who your business serves, and what your company is (or will be).

Mission statements are hard to write. They are more honest than an advertisement, more personal than a sales pitch, and a bit touchy-feely.

1. Start with your elevator pitch (see *Introduction*). Some experts believe that your mission statement should be very brief and easy to remember. Keep it as short as possible and never more than three or four sentences.

2. Write clearly and concisely for people who aren't in the food service industry.

3. Don't brag; just be straightforward and realistic.

4. Don't go overboard with superlatives, such as unequalled service or fabulous food.

5. Think about what you want your customers to receive from dining at your restaurant. For example:

    a. You want them to be physically and emotionally satisfied.

    b. You want them to experience the pleasures of quality food.

    c. You want them to have fun.

6. Look at sample statements of purpose for creative stimulus, but don't take one as your own as it simply won't capture the essence of your plan's message.

7. Read *Creating Mission Statements for Smaller Groups* by Beverly Goldberg ($3.95 PDF download at **www.amazon.com**).

Business Goals and Objectives

Your business goals and objectives will cover your short-term (within one year) and long-term (two to five years) expectations as a business and entrepreneur. Think of goals as your dreams with a deadline and your objectives as the way you will achieve those goals. Your goals are typically measured in dollars or other tangible results.

Common restaurant goals are:

1. Sales volume.

2. Hours owner(s) works.

3. Number of customers.

4. Profit levels.

5. Number of future employees.

6. Cash flow.

7. Expansion (additional stores or larger restaurant facility).

Objectives are the steps you will take to achieve these goals. These are measurable activities that answer the queries of who, what, how, why and when.

Who = Management team

What = Increase customer returns

How = Weekly customer service training

Why = Happier customers equals repeat customers

When = Three-month review and assessment

Your first goal—the launch of your new restaurant—is detailed below.

Short-Term

Goal #1—Official restaurant opening date of November 5.

- Hire general manager to assist with overseeing complete renovation of leased building.

- Hire general contractor with restaurant remodeling experience.

- Obtain $50,000 capital equipment loan.

Long-Term

Goal #5—Open second restaurant in local suburb in year three.

- Cash reserves of $150,000 to be set aside for expansion funding.

- Set monthly savings goals to raise additional $150,000 in eight months.

- Create training/mentoring program for assistant manager to be responsible for outfitting and starting second restaurant.

Start by creating three to five short-term goals and outline how you will achieve these. Be realistic and use your financial projections to benchmark and support your ability to reach each goal. Your objectives should be doable for a busy restaurant owner. It is okay to dream, but the purpose here is to set business and personal goals that are attainable and go beyond the normal daily requirements of being in business for yourself.

General Description of Business

Your business description is an expanded paragraph that details what your business does. Start again with your elevator pitch (see *Introduction*). It includes descriptions of the products (food, beverage, other) that you will offer, your concept (theme, formal/informal), your service style (dine-in, take-out), along with any other pertinent information that enables the reader to visualize your food service establishment. Your description can also include your legal business structure (corporation, partnership, sole proprietorship) and fiscal year (annual or other date). Your restaurant name—your brand name—will be revealed here. (*Chapter 6* discusses registering and developing your brand name.)

Below are two examples of business descriptions for food service establishments.

Example #1

> Arden Meadows will be a seasonal café, located next to Lake Arden, featuring BBQ and American cuisine. Customers will be seasonal visitors to the 250-square-mile Lake Arden public-use region including the Mt. Ray National Park (U.S. Forest Service-operated camping facilities). Operating from May 15 through September 30, the café while have an informal sunflower theme and outdoor dining areas. Picnic-style take-out and sit-down service will be available. An adjoining full-service bar operated by the Big Beer Company will provide Arden Meadows' customers with alcoholic beverages. Arden Meadows will be owned and operated by partners Jim Sweet and Fred Anderson as a Nevada limited liability corporation with a November 1–October 30 accounting period.

Example #2

> Fargo is a family friendly steakhouse with a historical Wild West theme located at the Smithridge Mall in Irvine, California, near Interstate 5. Open seven days a week, Fargo serves Southern California tourists and residents with family oriented entertainment including line dancing servers and classic country and western music. The menu features cowboy-style meals served family style in a rustic atmosphere including glass jars for mugs and tin plates as chargers. Owned and operated by the husband and wife partnership of Norman and Betty Paul, Fargo has shown a 35 percent annual pretax profits for the past six calendar years.

Your business description is your creation. You won't need to do any specific research to write this section. Look at sample business plans for other ideas on how to tell your story so a stranger would immediately know what your restaurant is like.

Description of Products/Services

Restaurants sell products—foods and beverages—and they sell services. For example, your business could offer 20-minute pizza delivery service, custom off-site catering or banquets. A good way to define what you will sell and what services you offer is to create a list of features (what you offer customers) and add the benefits your customers' will receive from each feature. Benefits are the what's-in-it-for-me part of marketing your products and services.

Here are a few examples of the features and benefits that a

café/bakery might offer customers.

Features	Benefits
Staff arrives very early for first shift.	Customers have plenty of time to stop by before work. Convenient times for local manufacturing plant workers on first shift.
Fresh-baked bagels, muffins and bread.	Convenient, great-tasting breakfast items for dine-in and take-out.
Custom-decorated cakes.	Easy to stop by and order a special occasion cake. Place order during breakfast and pick up after work.
Free coffee with any purchase.	Save money eating here.
Delivery service.	No one has to leave a business meeting or luncheon to feed guests.

Lists are a great way to get ideas on paper. Your lists can be a single word or an entire thought to explain the topic. Grab that notepad and let your mind go to create lists from which to write your product/service description section.

> List 1: To help you develop your niche—what you do best and promote most—create another list that answers the question, what makes your products and/or services unique or special?

List 2: How do you differ from your competitors? Are you higher priced? Do you offer take-out? Open longer? Write down every difference you can think of.

List 3: What special resources do you have going for you? This can be anything from name recognition within your community to outstanding chef awards to a patent or trademark.

List 4: How will you produce your product/service? Will everything be made in-house? What special equipment will be required?

List 5: Are there any obstacles or negatives associated with your products? Need air quality permit for charbroiler? Is your menu too foreign for your community? Will you need to rely on hard-to-locate items? Are there limited vendors capable of supplying you?

List 6: What products/services are in your future? Will you be able to respond to food trends? Will your customers want you to?

From Your Lists to Your Plan

The free-form nature of creating lists should reveal some good ideas and some great ones; concentrate on the great ones in your plan. Your first subsection is to describe in detail your products and services. You don't have to include recipes, but a sample menu is an appropriate support document.

Don't dismiss the off-the-wall ideas that appear on your lists. Some of the world's greatest innovations came to life because someone let their imagine soar.

Discuss specific ingredients, preparation and serving methods. Tell the reader how these set you apart from competitors, why they are desired by customers, and your profit potential. Good marketing focuses on the benefits to the customers, and your plan should likewise. No matter how excited about a specific product you are, unless it connects with patrons, it isn't a winner!

Your service (dining style, service levels, etc.) is also a critical part of your offerings and a way to set your business apart from the competition. Discuss how these affect the product quality, your customer needs and profitability. Don't forget to tie your service style/methods into your customer demographics. For example: if you have a café serving a tourist area at a lake, your take-out window conveniently situated for docked boats is a real asset.

Management Structure and Organization

In this section, you'll describe your legal form of business and ownership. Ownership percentages and participation requirements will be included here. Your accountant and/or attorney can advise on you the best form for your business to protect yourself from personal financial risks and for the greatest tax benefits. (For more information on business structures and do-it-yourself incorporation, see *Chapter 14 – Resources.*)

Below you will find a brief description of the business entities you can choose.

Sole Proprietorship — The easiest and least costly way of starting a business.

A sole proprietorship can be formed by simply finding a location and opening the door for business. Start-up attorney's fees will be less than those of other business forms. The owner has absolute authority over all business decisions. The biggest negative to a sole proprietorship is your personal liability should the business default on a loan or be involved in a legal dispute.

Partnership — Two or more parties that join together to share ownership.

The two most common partnership types are general and limited. A general partnership can be formed simply by an oral agreement between two or more persons, but a legal partnership agreement drawn up by an attorney is highly recommended. Legal fees for drawing up a partnership agreement are higher than those for a sole proprietorship, but may be lower than incorporating. A partnership agreement could be helpful in solving any disputes. However, partners are responsible for the other partner's business actions, as well as their own.

Corporation — Business entity where control depends upon stock ownership.

A business may incorporate without an attorney, but legal advice is highly recommended. The corporate structure is usually the most complex and is more costly to organize. Control depends on stock ownership. Persons with the largest stock ownership, not the total number of shareholders, control the corporation. Small, closely held corporations can operate more informally, but recordkeeping cannot be eliminated. Officers of a corporation can be liable to stockholders for improper actions. Liability is generally limited to stock ownership, except where fraud is involved. You may want to incorporate as a C or S corporation.

Limited Liability Company (LLC) — Blends the benefits of a corporation with a sole ownership or partnership.

The LLC is not a corporation, but it offers many of the same advantages. Many small-business owners and entrepreneurs prefer an LLC because they combine the limited liability protection of a corporation with the pass-through taxation of a sole proprietorship or partnership. An LLC has advantages over corporations that allow greater flexibility in management and business organization.

Your Management Team

Managing a business requires more than just the desire to be your own boss. It demands dedication, persistence, the capacity to make wise decisions and the ability to manage both employees and finances. Your management plan, along with your marketing and financial management sections, is your business foundation.

People are your greatest business resources and most valuable asset. To maximize your human resources, take a good look at the talents you possess and what skills you lack. Your job now is to hire personnel that can supply your missing skills.

You also need to look at what you do best and how that can best serve your business. Even if you can create a profit and loss statement or design a Web page, you need to consider if this is the best use of your time. Until there are more than 24 hours in a day, you'll need to invest your time in activities that earn money first. If you are the creative talent in the kitchen, don't be afraid to outsource or hire someone to handle the operational and support duties. Learn how to train people for advancement and delegate duties. Entrepreneurs often like to do it themselves or feel they are the only one who can do it; this is a self-limited managerial style. Share the duties and responsibilities and you'll have rewards to share also.

Your management plan should answer questions such as:

- How does your background/business experience help you in this business?

- What are your weaknesses and how can you compensate for them?

- Who will be on the management team?

- What are management's strengths/weaknesses? (Although you won't write directly about the weak spots in your team, they will be noticed by business professionals. Explain the missing skills before someone can question your team's ability.)

- What are their duties?

- Are these duties clearly defined?

- If a franchise, what type of assistance can you expect from the franchiser?

- Will this assistance be ongoing?

- What are your current personnel needs?

- What are your plans for hiring and training personnel?

- What salaries, benefits, vacations and holidays will you offer?

- If a franchise, will these issues be covered in the management package the franchiser will provide?

- How will you attract quality employees?

- How can you keep employees happy and productive?

- What benefits, if any, can you afford at this point?

If this is a franchise, the operating procedures, manuals and materials devised by the franchiser should be included in this section of the business plan. (If they are too bulky, simply list them by title and refer the reader to their location.) Lenders will consider the strength of the franchiser as part of your management capabilities. Study these documents carefully when writing your business plan and be sure to incorporate the important highlights. The franchiser should assist you with management training and ongoing management support.

Your Key Personnel

As the owner/operator of a small hot dog stand, you'll probably hold all the key positions in your company—owner, employee, accountant, personnel director. If your business is a solo operation, you'll be telling the reader what makes you capable of filling these roles.

If your food service establishment is significantly larger, you'll have a variety of key personnel to share the responsibility of daily operations, decision-making and supervision of people and things. Here is where you'll discuss the skills and expertise your key personnel bring to your business. For example, if you want to feature rich, elaborate European-style pastries, then your pastry chef's talents and experience are of great importance.

Key personnel in your restaurant could be:

- Operations Manager
- Head Chef
- Maitre d'
- Bookkeeper
- Partner
- Pastry Chef
- Wine Steward
- Catering Salesperson
- Banquet Manager
- Head Bartender
- Human Resources Manager

Outside Support

An owner or manager needs not handle all of the restaurant's fiscal and managerial responsibilities. Outside consultants and advisors can be a great way to enhance your management resources. Your accountant, lawyer, insurance broker, ad agency, PR firm, remodeling contractor, food service consultants, real estate broker, restaurant equipment salesperson and suppliers can all add depth to your management capabilities.

Management Philosophy

Your management style indicates how you make decisions, how you delegate and how you interact with personnel. You won't need to say, "I am an easy boss to get along with"; but you should talk about your team-building philosophy or other work ethics that support your mission statement.

Organizational Chart

Depending upon the size of your organization (personnel), you can either include a chart or just describe who will be reporting to whom. Organizational or flow charts can be created using Chart/Diagram functions of Microsoft Word. Charts and diagrams can also be created in PowerPoint and Excel.

The Next Three Big Sections

The next three sections of your plan—Marketing, Financial Data and Feasibility Study—are the most detailed and complex. The Marketing section is really a plan within a plan. Marketing plans can also be created separately for internal purposes instead of a full business plan. The information provided in your financial section shows your ability to pay for your business requirements and make a profit. Your feasibility study is your report on the ability to accomplish your restaurant's economic goals. I'll discuss these in full detail in the following three chapters. If you wish to follow the plan outline, move on to *Chapters 6, 7 and 8*, then return here to complete your written plan.

Coming to a Conclusion

Your conclusion isn't just the end of your written business plan. It is a recap of the points you made that prove your plan to be viable and profitable. Your conclusion is also your opportunity to ask for what you want and tell them why.

I am seeking an additional $50,000 in loans to complete the renovation of the historical Adams building. This represents 15 percent of the funds needed for this project and would provide Provencal with six additional tables.

Support Documents

This section includes various personal financial documents, legal documents and other items that support your statements within the plan. Examples are listed below. You may have other documents that you feel will give your lender or investor additional information of importance.

1. Personal tax returns of the principals (owners) for the last three years.

2. Business tax returns for the last three years (if you are already operational).

3. Personal financial statements for each principal detailing your assets and liabilities.

4. Copy of franchise contracts and documents supplied by the franchiser (if applicable).

5. Copy of proposed lease or purchase agreement for building space and/or land.

6. Copy of licenses and other legal documents.

7. Copy of resumés of all principals.

8. Copy of resumés of key employees.

9. Copies of letters of intent from suppliers, etc.

Note: Never attach originals unless they can be easily reproduced.

Let's Jump Back

Earlier in this chapter, I skipped over the marketing, financial sections and feasibility sections due to the amount of information that needs to be covered. *Chapter 6* discusses preparing your feasibility study. *Chapter 7* outlines your restaurant's marketing from analysis of competitors to advertising campaigns. *Chapter 8* guides you through the financial information you'll need to share.

6

Writing a Feasibility Analysis

Feasibility is the likelihood that something can be carried out or achieved. A feasibility study covers the physical, emotional, financial and market needs of your business idea and answers the big question: Should I start (or expand) a food service business? Many aspects of a feasibility study and analysis overlap with your business plan; however, they have different functions. Your feasibility study is your confirmation that your idea has sufficient merit to create your business plan—with the emphasis on planning. Think of a feasibility analysis as an exploration of your ideas and your business plan as a plan for action.

Your restaurant's study is a critical decision-making tool for you, your partners and your lender. The analysis can also be a financial lifesaver allowing you to revise your vision and improve its potential for success before you invest your financial future.

After reading this chapter, you may decide that your first step should be to conduct a feasibility study, as much of the information gathered for the feasibility analysis can be used to write your formal business plan.

Start by reading over your plan, looking at your projected numbers and examining your self-determination. Before putting anything on paper in this section, you'll need to determine for yourself whether your restaurant idea is financially, physically and emotionally achievable in the real world. It is important that you are honest with yourself; slanting the outcome towards profitability means that you aren't facing business realities — not all ideas are moneymakers and not everyone is cut out to be an entrepreneur.

1. Can it be profitable?

2. Will people come?

3. Do I have the desire to be successful?

4. Am I willing to work hard for little pay?

5. Do I have sufficient financial resources to sustain my family and business until I become profitable?

If the answers to these questions are yes, you are ready to create your written feasibility analysis.

Hiring a Study Consultant

Your accountant or an outside consulting firm can prepare your feasibility study. They would take your in-progress business plan, conduct some additional research, review your financial data, consider your assumptions, and prepare a formal written study. You can expect to pay from $500 for a basic feasibility review of your plan to $4,500 for a comprehensive study.

You'll find business consultants with restaurant experience on the Web by searching for "restaurant feasibility study" or "food service consultants." You'll find helpful tips on hiring a consultant in *Chapter 3 – Hiring a Business Plan Writer*.

Preparing Your Analysis

Your analysis must be based upon thorough research and fact-based assumptions. As you research the categories below, think about the questions people would ask you before deciding whether to loan you money, invest in your ideas, become a partner or accept a job.

Your feasibility analysis should give you a clear picture of your:

1. Needs — Must-haves that are the foundation of your concept and success.

2. Wants — Desirable elements that will make life easier, increase profits or save money.

3. Wishes — Features that you'd love to have but aren't

important to your launch or short-term ability to grow your business.

Your analysis will cover your:

1. Concept—Your theme, service style, menu, customer needs and competition.

2. Location—Its convenience, accessibility, visibility and proximity to your customer base.

3. Execution—How you will make it real.

4. Financing Needs—What will it cost to start or grow a profitable restaurant?

Concept Analysis

In reviewing the potential of your concept, you will be asking and answering a variety of quantitative questions. Are the numbers there to support your idea? Is your community struggling economically? Do dining trends support your growth assumptions?

In analyzing the feasibility of your concept, you'll be reviewing food service industry statistics, local economic conditions, community growth potential, customer demographics and consumer patterns.

Look at the data you've gather to determine:

1. **The meals people eat out most often.** Do potential patrons only eat breakfast out on weekends? Are competitors busiest during lunch hours? Are locals interested in lingering after work?

2. **Traffic patterns around your location.** Are there natural commuting patterns that go past your restaurant? Are you located in a destination spot that will bring people to your door? Is there easy access or must they do a U-turn to get to you?

3. **The economic health of your community.** Everyone needs to eat, but dining out is a discretionary activity directly affected for economic ups and downs. Is your community growing? Are businesses shutting down?

4. **Seasonal conditions.** Do you have a seasonal population fluctuation? Are you near a tourist destination? Will people be interested in heavy, comfort food during your long, hot summer months?

5. **Spending history and patterns.** Are locals spending their dining-out dollars at fast-food joints or upscale dinner houses? Can your potential customers afford your offerings?

The key question to answer is "Does my restaurant concept fit with what I know about my community, customers and competitors?" For example, if you are locating in a bedroom community where people drive by on their way out of town and never stop for breakfast, would a pancake house be a wise venture?

Location Analysis

Where your restaurant lives is of critical importance. It can be a costly mistake or the starting point for a profitable chain. Some entrepreneurs focus their entire feasibility study on this single issue. You'll want to look carefully at the pluses and minuses of:

- Leasing a stand-alone building.

- Leasing a single unit in an industrial complex or shopping mall.

- Subletting a small space in an office building or mall courtyard.

- Renovating a historical building.

- Purchasing an existing restaurant.

- Building a brand new store.

Your analysis should confirm your location is:

1. **Where the customers are.**

a. Are there ample sources of customers? Are there hungry employees nearby? Do other businesses attract people to your neighborhood? Will tourist business be enough to keep you afloat during off-season?

b. Will you have to reach customers outside your immediate community to fill your seats? Expecting patrons to travel across town past six competitive steakhouses is a recipe for insufficient sales. Yes, restaurants can draw patrons from around the world but it takes time to build that type of buzz and an enormous investment in creative talent, atmosphere and advertising.

2. **Needed.**

a. Is your area underserved by all food establishments? Are people having to stand too long to be served? Are there overflow crowds? Is the drive-up always busy?

b. Are people hungry for your food offerings? Do they crave it?

c. Is your concept unique in your community? Could it be too trendy? Could people become quickly bored with your concept?

d. Can you take customers from your competition? Will you be able to entice people to dine out more frequently?

3. **Where and how your customers would want to find you.**

a. Are you near when the hunger pangs strike?

b. Are you easy to find and reach? Would it be easier to drive another block so diners don't have to make a dangerous left-hand turn? Would customers rather go to the competitor's drive-up window instead of coming inside your establishment?

c. Will people forget you're there because you are in an unusual location?

4. **Competitively balanced.** A healthy competitive environment can be a good thing. That's why you'll often find multiple fast-food establishments located near busy intersections. Areas without any competition should be a red flag signaling a potentially inadequate customer base or economic limitations. If your competition looks healthy and busy, your restaurant's need factor increases significantly.

Have Concept, Need Location

As the cliché goes, it's location, location, location. Perhaps you've got your concept finalized and haven't selected a location yet—your study can help you in your search for the perfect location and help you get past mental roadblocks that keep you from launching your new restaurant. There are only so many perfect locations and the high demand may make them unaffordable, so studying the feasibility of multiple locations can keep you on track and on budget.

Have Location, Need Concept

If you have found the right location to purchase, build upon or lease, your feasibility study can focus in on everything from handicap accessibility issues to food service zoning.

Should I Buy Someone Else's Restaurant?

Sometimes the best location is already somebody else's. If you are considering purchasing an existing food service establishment, your feasibility study should review its location potential and its true value (as opposed to the purchase price) for your business. Can you save money on equipment? Are there negatives associated with the existing establishment? Will your remodeling needs overwhelm any potential financial benefits?

If you have taken time to do some personal reflection, compared your resources to your needs, and set realistic expectations, you'll be better prepared to build, buy or lease your restaurant, launch a new business and create a foundation for success and profits. The following worksheet is a helpful assessment tool to determine which way of starting a business best suits you.

GOING INTO BUSINESS

(This form can be used to tally pluses and minuses or to make comments.)

Factors	From Scratch	Buy Existing Business	Franchise
Time			
Availability			
Launch Time (planning to opening)			
Financial			
Cost			
Available Financing			
Investors			
Personal Worth Requirements			
Total Indebtedness			
Break-Even Point			
Royalties & Fees			
Purchasing Restrictions			
Current Profitability			

Intangibles			
Goodwill			
Historical Recognition			
Known vs. Unknown (obstacles to success or existing profitability)			
Reputation			
Convenience			
Exclusivity			
Assets			
Location			
Facility			
Equipment			
Existing Staff			
Customer Base			

Owner			
Independence			
Business Experience			
Food Service Experience			
Management Experience			
Owner Expectations			
Outside Expectations			
Training			
Support			
Marketshare			
Marketing Support			
Product Mix			
Competition			
Customer Needs			
Other (your personal list)			

Execution Analysis

Execution analysis is the form your restaurant idea takes and the steps you must take to create a healthy business. How your idea manifests itself is a combination of your dreams, your customers' needs and competitive influences. Your execution analysis goes deeper than reviewing your concept, it looks at:

1. How you can fine-tune your idea based upon your customer needs, competition and market conditions research.

2. The financial results of your decisions including various changes to your original concept.

3. How you'll capture market share (advertising and PR).

4. Potential problem areas and their solutions.

5. Your ability to be a successful owner and operator of a food service establishment.

Fine-Tuning Your Idea

Whether you are starting your first restaurant or considering major changes to an active business, working through various scenarios can help you determine its profit potential. As you learn more about your customers, you'll be able to fine-tune your idea to better serve them.

For example, let's say you want to open a sandwich shop. You could 1) be open for lunch only, 2) add a few breakfast sandwiches and gourmet coffee and open at 7 a.m., or 3) close at 9 p.m. when nearby stores close. By charting out on an hourly basis your sales, costs and customer potential, you can decide what is best for your customers and your bottom line.

The following chart below illustrates this type of analysis (the numbers used are for demonstration purpose only). Notice that by adding breakfast, your hourly profit declines significantly, because your customer-per-hour figure declines. Coffee (primarily purchased in the morning) is a highly profitable item but the lower profit margin on breakfast items had a negative impact.

However, when you add dinner hours where customers purchase more desserts and snacks, your profits more than double! Perhaps customers are hungrier later in the day or more people stop by for an afternoon break. Looking at the whys can also help you focus on your most profitable items.

Open Weekdays Only	Lunch Only	Breakfast and Lunch	Breakfast, Lunch and Dinner
Hours Open	3 hours (11 a.m. to 2 p.m.)	6 hours (7 a.m. to 2 p.m.)	14 hours (7 a.m. to 9 p.m.)
Customers Served	280	480	1,275
Customers per Hour (avg.)	93	80	91
Average Check per Person	$5.45	$4.99 (breakfast items are less expensive)	$6.75 (more desserts and snacks sold)
Daily Sales	**$1,526.00**	**$2,395.20**	**$8,606.25**
Cost of Goods Sold (per customer)	$3.25	$3.00	$3.40
Daily Cost of Goods Sold	$910.00	$1,440.00	$4,335.00
Hourly Overhead Factor	$29.00	$29.00	$38.00
Daily Overhead Costs (includes 30 minutes prep and clean-up)	$116.00	$203.00	$570.00
Daily Profit Potential	**$500.00**	**$752.20**	**$3,701.25**
Profit per Customer	$1.79	$1.57	$2.90
Profit per Hour Opened	$166.67	$125.33	$264.38

Financing Needs

"Money makes the world go 'round." A financial feasibility analysis looks at how much money it takes to accomplish a goal and whether it will pay for itself; while your financial report section of your business plan looks at the anticipated view of your financial future.

When looking at financial scenarios, you'll consider factors such as hours of operation, average check per person, seat turnover and number of customers. We looked at hours of operation as a factor in the prior chart. In addition, notice that the average check per person changed based upon the various meal times. By reviewing your costs and overhead, you can estimate your average check size and compare that with food service industry statistics available through national and state restaurant associations.

Seat turnover is how many times each seat is occupied by a different customer during a meal period. If you have 100 seats and you serve 300 people during dinner hours, you have three turns per seat ($300 \div 100 = 3$). The Restaurant Industry Operations Report prepared annually by the National Restaurant Association can give you some benchmark figures to work with. Turnover rates will vary by mealtime, day of the week and month. You may need to more than one turnover rate to achieve a more accurate picture in projecting sales and cash flow.

Does It Make Good Fiscal Sense?

Financial feasibility studies also look at various scenarios and weigh the benefits against the cost of borrowing or investing. For example, the following chart compares the cost of increased seating capacity against the cost of building and outfitting this space. The facts are merely for demonstration purposes. Increasing seating capacity by 20 seats has the lowest return and takes longer to pay for itself. Depending upon your cash flow, either the 36- or 52-seat addition could be a good one.

Seating Capacity	20 Additional	36 Additional	52 Additional
Monthly Sales Increase	$10,000.00	$18,000.00	$28,000.00
Additional Cost of Goods Sold	$5,900.00	$10,620.00	$16,520.00
Additional Monthly Overhead	$3,120.00	$4,520.00	$6,555.00
Additional Profit	**$980.00**	**$2,860.00**	**$4,925.00**
Cost for Expansion	$18,000.00	$25,200.00	$39,000.00
Cost Outfitting Space	$ 5,500.00	$7,500.00	$10,000.00
Total cost	$23,500.00	$32,700.00	$49,000.00
Pays for Itself	**In 24 months**	**In 12 months**	**In 10 months**

Capturing Your Fair Share

There are literally hundreds of ways to market your restaurant and capture a share of the dining dollar. The feasibility study of your advertising and promotion compares the cost of each campaign, the medium and potential customers reached. It also weighs these costs against your anticipated sales increase. Besides comparing the different types of marketing activities, you'll also need to consider competitive influences.

Another competitive decision (also considered a marketing activity) is your pricing structure. What will the market bear? What are competitors charging? Should you focus on lower profit margins and greater volume? What will it cost you in profits, reputation and quality to be the low-price leader? How will differentiating your business through advertising help you maintain higher pricing?

You can create feasibility comparison "what if" scenarios such as:

1. If I lower my price by 75 cents, how much more do I have to sell each day to recoup the loss?

2. If I raise my price by $2.00 but lose two customers a day, can I still be profitable?

3. If my radio ad costs me $500 a week, how many customer visits must I add each week to break even? Increase sales?

4. If I offer a Buy-1-Get-1-Free coupon, how many new customers must come in before I earn back what it costs me?

5. If I accept my competitors' coupons, how many new customers must I capture to pay for the promotion?

Problems and Solutions

As you research and explore your restaurant concept, the market and your competition, you may discover problem areas. No business idea is 100 percent foolproof, so analyzing potential solutions can prepare you for battle. Look for ways to calculate the best solution(s) for your potential problems, whether those are new competition, zoning obstacles or lack of qualified employees.

The first step in exploring potential problems is to define them. Let's use the example of Juan's House of Burritos and how Juan might address a competitive problem. A popular Mexican restaurant chain is going to be locating nearby in four months. With national recognition and a budget to match, the competitor could literally wipe out Juan. Juan needs to look at:

- How will it affect his business?

- What are the financial impacts?

- How much loss can he bear and stay profitable?

- Will it cost him more to compete?

- How can he increase his visibility?

- How can he sell his differences?

- How can he reward current customers and keep them coming back?

- How much money will it take to advertise more?

While many business decisions aren't solely based on dollars and cents, equating problems to a what-will-it-cost-me figure gives you a tangible way to measure its impact. Look at the bottom line and then factor in such issues as:

1. Will it be harder to keep good employees?

2. Will my staff be happy?

3. Will customers notice the difference?

4. Are there enough hours in the day to do it myself?

5. Will spending more help me earn more?

Entrepreneurs Aren't Superheroes

New entrepreneurs may have an abundance of passion but lack the managerial skills, business savvy or food service experience necessary for success. Restaurants have a higher than average failure rate so a strong management team is critical. This is your opportunity to explore your own abilities and experience before starting a risky venture. After analyzing your restaurant's management strengths and weaknesses, you'll be better prepared to deal with the scrutiny of lenders and investors.

A feasibility analysis of you — the restaurateur and your staff — is not a matter of numbers (except when it comes to budgeting salaries); it is an assessment of your combined ability to run a successful restaurant. Start your management study by creating a list of the various duties that your key personnel must handle. They will fall into five broad categories.

1. **Kitchen Management** — Examples are profitable menu development, sanitation regulation compliance, food cost control, back-of-the-house operations.

2. **Operations** — Examples are building maintenance, front-of-the-house operations, sanitation regulation compliance, facility/customer interaction.

3. **Personnel** — Examples are hiring, training, supervising, motivating and firing employees, employee law and company policy compliance, employee manual development.

4. **Finance** — Examples are daily bookkeeping, bank reconciliation, payroll, daily/weekly/monthly sales and profits reports, analysis of financial activities, taxes.

5. **Marketing** — Examples are customer retention programs, media buys, public relations, Web development, menu design/production, advertising.

Your list may have other duties that a manager will need to handle personally or must supervise. Your key personnel may not have managerial titles, but often carry out managerial tasks.

When a lender or investor is assessing your potential for success, they will be reviewing your ability to manage critical areas of your restaurant. If your proposed operation is a small one, you may be the entire management staff. Partnerships can share the responsibilities and larger operations should seek to have experienced personnel capable of handling these also.

In assessing your management team, you should start with yourself. If you had to do every one of the tasks outlined, could you? Then review whether you should — Is this a good use of my time and talents? Can I hire an employee to do this or outsource this to a consultant, advisor or other professional?

For those who will be the entire management team; the good news is that you can outsource a great majority of items on your list. Some items are typically best left to a professional (such as taxes and financial analysis) and others are infrequent activities (such as media buys) where a full-time employee isn't necessary. Before doing it yourself, do some research. In some cases, paying an expert can actually save you money!

Look closely at the weaknesses of your staff. Your analysis will help you determine the people you need to hire or outsource to build a strong management team. As you write employee job descriptions, think about finding these missing talents and skills. When interviewing, ask about hidden talents and experience that can also be tapped.

If you'll be supporting your business with consulting services, address it in your business plan similar to the following examples.

- The accounting firm of Smith, Goodman and Ott will be handling all financial matters.

- Suzy Amis of DreamMakers will be providing public relations services.

- Our bookkeeping department will be working with Samuel Wanamaker, CPA.

Armed with your feasibility analysis on management and supervisory capabilities, you can share the positives and provide solutions for the negatives. Talk about all the talents (creative, people-friendly), skills (baking expert), education (hospitality degree) and experience (15 years working for the best restaurant in town) you have as resources.

Not Enough Strength

Perhaps your analysis will reveal that your personal expertise and background isn't broad enough to operate your dream restaurant successfully. If you simply cannot afford to hire a larger staff or outside service provider, you will need to contemplate your options. Here are a few things you might consider:

1. Delay your plans and acquire the skills that are missing by returning to school or taking a job where you can learn firsthand.

2. Find a mentor. The missing ingredients to success are not always predictors of failure—you can (and should) learn as you go with the guidance of a mentor.

3. Look for a business partner with the missing ingredient. He or she can share the financial risks and the rewards along with dividing up the managerial duties.

No matter what this study reveals, you must look at its results as another smart move on your part. You've armed yourself with excellent decision-making information.

Do I Need It and Can I Afford It?

When starting a brand new restaurant, you have to weigh your dreams against its costs. This is especially true for food service equipment! Wandering through a food service supply house can really make your mouth water. Beautiful, shiny stainless steel…powerful motors…fancy tools! But wait! Do you really need it and can you afford it?

Studying the feasibility of purchasing tangible items (equipment, vehicles and buildings) can help you focus on the reality instead of the dream. This is financial analysis and will require you to do some comparative shopping between manufacturers, models, new and used.

Here are some of the questions you need to be answering:

1. Would it be more cost-effective to purchase an existing restaurant?

2. Could becoming a franchisee of a well-respected chain give me free resources?

3. Will remodeling make good fiscal sense or should I move to a new location?

4. Do I really need that $5,000 espresso machine or should I take the free one from the coffee vendor?

5. Can I find a quality used piece of equipment or must I buy a new one?

6. Will a less expensive brand or model have the same longevity as the one I really want?

7. Is this purchase a wish, want or must have?

8. What would it cost me in time or money savings if I didn't have this laborsaving device?

The following example will give you an idea on how to determine whether a new dishwasher is a better purchase than a used one. Both units have the same capacity and cycle time so output is equal. Electricity and water usage are also equal. You would need to factor in these should the equipment you are comparing vary. For example, in a very busy restaurant slower units may require you to invest in more dinnerware. The manufacturers' specification sheets will provide you with these figures. Energy consumption data and analysis information is also available from the federal government at **www.energystar.gov**. Depreciation factors will also affect the results slightly.

New Dishwasher	Used Dishwasher
$9,000 investment	$4,000 investment
5-year warranty on parts and 1 year on labor	90-day warranty (parts and labor)
New model – all parts available	Discontinued model – parts may be limited

10-year lifespan	6-year lifespan
$900 repair costs in 10 years	$2,500 repair costs in 6 years
Equipment cost— $990 per year	Equipment cost— $1,083.33 per year
$200 per month consumables (detergent and rinse aid)	$250 per month consumables (detergent and rinse aid)
$3,390 annual ownership cost	$2,883.33 annual ownership cost
$282.50 monthly ownership cost	$240.28 Monthly ownership cost

Although the new dishwasher should last four years longer and saves $50 a month on consumables, the used one has a significantly lower annual ownership cost. Saving $5,000 upfront makes sense too!

Tip: When considering a dishwasher purchase, you might also consider a dishwasher rental program. National companies such as Auto-Chlor and Rykoff offer very cost-effective programs when you purchase their detergents and there are no maintenance costs.

Do-It-Yourself Feasibility Studies

There are plenty of qualified restaurant consultants to do feasibility studies. Many business plan writers can also provide these services. Once again, doing it yourself gives you numerous benefits. Many of these feasibility studies are for internal use so how they look isn't important — it's what they prove (or disprove) that counts. However, you may find that providing a brief written analysis within your full business plan can support your project's feasibility.

Writing Your Feasibility Analysis

Your feasibility analysis should tell readers in strong words what your study proves. Two or three concise paragraphs are plenty. Below is an example of integrating a study's results.

> Based on two months of traffic flow data gathering, we have isolated the potentially most productive hours for Toscana. At this time, there is insufficient foot or vehicle traffic to warrant being open during lunch hours. Our operating hours will be 4:30 p.m. to 9 p.m., Monday through Thursday. Extended hours (until 11:30 p.m.) will be offered on Friday and Saturday nights because of our proximity to a thriving movie theater.

Refer to your financial studies as proof that your plan is feasible. Sentences like, "In year two, the restaurant will have recouped its initial start-up investment as illustrated in report 4B," or "Based on the current dining trends and our increased customer capacity, we will have ample sales volume and profits to cover all outstanding loans and payables within the 36-month loan period. See report #4 on page 22."

Your feasibility analysis should also include your needs. If your business plan is solid and you have established an ability to repay a loan or give an investor a reasonable return on their investment, you should tell them that here. If you are asking for funding support (loans or investments), discuss how this will positively affect your outcome. "The additional capital will allow us to expand our current dining facilities by 100 percent. Based upon our historical patron turnover ratios, the repayment period would be less than the two-year length of the loan."

Feasibility studies that can be translated into financial reports will be part of your plan's financial section. These reports will need to be in a standard accounting format. Your accountant, accounting software or a book like *Accounting for Dummies* by John A. Tracy can show you what these reports should look like.

A great resource on feasibility studies (besides this book) is available from the National Restaurant Association. *Conducting a Feasibility Study for a New Restaurant* covers conducting competitive research, developing your concept and preparing your financial statement. The book is available at **www.restaurant.org** or by calling 800-424-5156, extension 5375.

Your Software Can Help

Be sure to review the feasibility analysis spreadsheets in your business plan writing software. Other assistance is available on line from RRG Consulting (www.rrgconsulting.com) in their free restaurant start-up and feasibility spreadsheets.

What to Do if the Answers Are Negative

It is quite possible that after spending weeks researching and writing your plan that the answers to these questions are that you are not ready to launch your dream or that your profit potential is too weak.

You have three choices. You can proceed with caution, rework your plan or move on to something else.

1. **Proceed with caution.** This can be a risky affair but businesses have been successful in spite of plans being dismissed as undoable. While attending Yale, Federal Express founder Fredrick W. Smith detailed his ideas for the world-famous delivery service in a poorly received paper. As the saying goes, the rest is history!

   If your plan has flaws, financial professionals will notice. Outside financing may be out of the question. This means that you will have to shoulder 100 percent of the burden and risks. Don't let your passion for your project cloud your judgment. Go into it with eyes wide open and never exceed your personal risk tolerance.

   Risk tolerance is your ability to handle being at risk emotionally, physically and financially. Think about various worst-case scenarios and determine just how much risk you are prepared to accept. A low-risk tolerance means you might want to rethink your plan.

To learn more about risk-taking,

- Visit Positive Way Business Solutions at **www.positive-way.com/business**.

- Read *Right Risk: 10 Powerful Principles for Taking Giant Leaps with Your Life* by Bill Treasurer.

2. **Rework your plan.** You can rework your plan and solve problems. If your dream hasn't diminished, use the information you have gathered and regroup. Look at its weak spots closely. Find areas within your plan that you can revise to overcome obstacles. For example, relocating your restaurant to a different part of town could mean a very long commute for you, but it might also mean less competition and a greater number of potential patrons.

   Chapter 12 – Revising and Updating Your Plan discusses how to revise your plan should you discover problems with your business idea.

3. **Move on.** You've explored your dreams, spent countless hours researching and writing your plan, not to mention the money you've invested. Now you are faced with the realization that your idea simply won't fly. Don't beat yourself up! Remember that the time, effort and money you invested in pursuing your dream is not a waste. Here is what you've gained from the process:

- **Better entrepreneurial skills.** You'll have learned new things that can make you a better businessperson.

- **The wisdom to know when you are wrong.** Many a businessperson has led their entire company off a cliff because they didn't recognize they were wrong. This is an invaluable decision-making skill.

- **The knowledge that you do have what it takes.** A good businessperson doesn't proceed when all the red flags are waving.

- **The start of a new business plan.** Steal sentences, paragraphs and complete sections for your next business venture's plan. True entrepreneurs are always dreaming of building their own business. Keep moving forward until the idea you have fulfills your financial dreams too.

- **Ideas on how to improve yourself.** If your dream derailed because you don't have enough managerial experience, find a class or become a trainee and work your way up. Do whatever it takes to make yourself worth investing in.

7

Your
Marketing Plan

Marketing is more than just how you'll advertise your restaurant. Marketing covers everything from the number of people who might visit your restaurant, to your competition to your pricing and charitable activities. Your marketing plan will define your industry, discuss trends, outline the need you will fill, create a target customer, and examine your competitions' weak spots.

Market Analysis

A marketing analysis looks at issues such as food and health trends, competitive influences, economic conditions and population characteristics that affect your sales volume. Analysis is really a series of questions you ask and answer through research that supports your claims.

The Food Service Industry

You'll start this portion of your business plan by discussing the food service industry along with the specific information on the segment within the industry that applies to your restaurant type.

The National Restaurant Association, federal government and other trade organizations can provide you with data and statistics on the restaurant industry. If you want to open a pizza parlor, statistics on coffee shops won't be on target.

When you detail the food service industry, you'll need to determine whether:

1. Your food offerings will be in or out (trends).

2. People will be dining out more or less (counts).

3. Health concerns will keep people away or bring them in (organic ingredients, low-carb diets or Mad Cow disease scares).

4. Competition will increase (independents or chain restaurants).

5. Populations will shift (people move in or away, age, have children or die).

6. Economic forecasts predict limited dining budgets (sales volume and check size).

7. Speed vs. service importance views shift (alters service styles).

Talk about the long-term prospects for the restaurant industry and for your type of restaurant. Address potential social and economic changes that will impact the food service industry. For example, the aging of America is a significant demographic change. How will this affect your menu offerings? facility? location? décor?

Your Territory

Your first step would be to take a local map and outline the neighborhoods surrounding your proposed (or existing) location. You can also select commercial areas where you'll draw workers from and popular commuting routes that bring hungry people past your door. Place bold dots where your competitors are located so that you can view the marketplace and how it is served.

Once you've determined your geographical territory, you can obtain demographic data that describes what people live and work in that area. Demographic data includes:

1. Affluence—discretionary income for dining out or budget-wise fast food.

2. Ages—young or elderly.

3. Marital status—single or married.

4. Family size—married with children, single-parent families.

5. Gender—male or female.

6. Ethnicity—how they affect food preferences, cultural habits and expectations.

7. Sexual orientation—gay and lesbian singles/couples.

8. Education levels—high school grads or advanced degrees.

9. Local wage levels—professionals or working class.

10. Seasonal or stable population—tourist influx, volume cycles.

11. Lifestyle preferences—where do the locals like to dine?

Your Location

Where you place your business directly affects your customers' ability to frequent it. In *Chapter 6 – Feasibility Studies,* I discuss analyzing location options. Various analyses could support such claims as how relocating can increase your customer traffic, why new construction would be more cost-effective than a major renovation or why a specific mall (although more costly to lease) is best suited to your restaurant concept. In *Chapter 9 – Researching Your Plan,* you'll find resources and advice on how to locate, select and acquire the location you'll need to be successful.

In this section of your business plan, you'll describe why your chosen location and the facilities work for you and your customers. If your plan is seeking money for an expansion, you'll be detailing why the location could support the cost of an expansion and the investment value of increasing your facility's capacity. If you are buying bare land and are seeking construction financing, provide complete information on the land, zoning and building design.

Your feasibility studies may reveal that owning your own physical space requires too much start-up capital or would create too great of an initial debt burden. Your dream location may be part of a larger complex. Your customers may want to find you in a mall, in an office building or sharing space with other complementary businesses. That means you'll be leasing.

Your contractual obligations, along with your lease rate and including rate, increase provisions, or lessor-provided benefits will be discussed here.

A long-term lease can be an advantage (stable expense and ability to build a local customer base) and a disadvantage (inability to relocate to accommodate a booming or declining business). Emphasize how leasing benefits your immediate financial situation and how you will deal with increased rates, exit clauses or renewal potential.

Your Competition

Rarely is there an idea that is without competition. Your restaurant will have a variety of businesses competing for your customers' dining dollar. You'll have competitors who sell the same type of food in the same type of atmosphere (all Italian pizzerias), competitors who offer the same type of food but with different service styles (take out vs. dine in), and other businesses where people purchase ready-to-eat meals.

Your direct competitors can be either the restaurants within a specific dining-in or take-it-home area around your store or those who offer the same food (all steakhouses in the community). Indirect competitors are other types of restaurants and stores that people might choose for take-out or dine-in meals instead of visiting your restaurant. Convenience has become a major decision-making factor for busy families. The ready-to-eat meal category within convenience stores and grocery stores has grown significantly over the past few years.

You'll need to compile a list of businesses that can (or do) have the greatest competitive affect on your food service establishment. Analyzing their strengths and weaknesses will give you insight into ways to outperform them and find a specific customer need that isn't being well served. Your competitive analysis can also help you justify the marketing efforts you feel you'll need to undertake to capture your share of hungry patrons.

Your research and analysis of the competition is critical to assessing your potential for success. You'll have to find paying customers in two ways: 1) by drawing in those who don't regularly eat your type of food, and 2) by taking customers away from the competition.

Your Customers

Without paying customers, there is simply no reason to open your doors. A powerful tool in developing your restaurant marketing concept is to create a customer(s) profile based upon geographic, demographic and economic data and personal observations.

Profiles are descriptions of your ideal customer and demonstrate that they are located within your service area. You'll also need to discuss why you are selecting a specific location, whether your food and service style meet the expectations of customers and how this affects your pricing structure.

Your Ideal Customer

By ideal customer, I am referring to an imaginary person who would like your restaurant, appreciate your food and return frequently. Looking at the population in your community will help you define this person by average age, economic status, gender, family size, transportation method and more.

- Your target restaurant/bar customer might be a young professional, most likely male, with above-average income, driving a sports car, nice dresser who dines out three to four nights a week.

- Your target fast-food restaurant customer might be

young families (single parent?) with children under the age of 12, rushing home after work, needing a fast to-go meal that can be consumed at home at value pricing.

- Your typical salad bar customer might be female, 22–45, who visits before shopping, dresses elegant casual, and looks for healthy choices but still interested in ample proportions.

- Your desired coffee shop customer might be on vacation at a nearby major resort area, mostly weekend visits, dresses according to season (skiwear or sun wear) interested in leisurely dining featuring local specialties; dessert is a must!

By defining your ideal customer(s), you'll have a mental image on which to build your restaurant. You'll know whom you should talk to in your advertising, the type of décor that would attract them, and the food they'd like to find in your restaurant.

Your Customers' Needs

This section is an assessment of what customer needs your restaurant will be filling. For example: you are opening a coffee shop/café that caters to the local theater crowd because there are no late-night dining venues in the area or you are opening a fast-food restaurant next to a high school full of hungry teens.

Establishing the Need

Your products and services should be developed and presented to customers as a solution to their needs. People need to eat for survival; however, when it comes to dining out, their needs go beyond hunger pangs. Here are some needs (physical, emotional and financial) that your patrons have:

- **Hunger** — physical hunger.

- **Cravings** — an emotional need (hunger) for a specific food.

- **Convenience** — easy to buy, minimal hassles, come-as-you-are dining.

- **Affordable** — pricing that fits customers' perceived value and/or budget.

- **Stress-relief** — provides relief for hunger while making life easier for customers juggling multiple demands, one less thing to worry about.

- **Pleasure** — entertainment, great tastes, refreshing beverages, comfortable surroundings that reward people.

- **Attention** — a way to show off, demonstrate class or wealth, to see and be seen by others and dining out as a reward (self-attention).

- **Fellowship**—a place for people to meet, to share conversations over drinks and a meal, a dating destination.

- **Protection**—food safety, quality, nutritional value, warding off fear for self and family.

Your Solutions

The second half of the need/solution equation is how you will satisfy your customers' needs. These should be posed as solutions. To follow are some suggestions on how you might present yourself as the solution to your customers' needs.

1. As a restaurant, you serve food—so you can satisfy your customers' hunger pangs. Fill the mind with ways to fill their stomachs.

2. Cravings arise from memories of smells, tastes, sights and good times and become a need that must be satisfied. While these are personal emotions, food trends often follow these cravings such as comfort foods (meatloaf and macaroni and cheese casseroles) during stressful times.

3. Convenience can mean location, style of service, hours of operation and delivery service. Make it easy to buy with credit cards/ATM or pump up your service to reduce wait times.

4. Affordable means different things to different people.

Does your food pricing fit in with the economic picture of your community? Affordable also means more than rock-bottom pricing; it means perceived value. For some people, a $9 burger with all the trimmings would be perfectly acceptable; for others they would feel that they were being robbed! Is the price appropriate for the quality of ingredients? Does your customer service add value to the meal?

5. Hungry kids, busy schedules, frustrating traffic delays are all part of modern-day stress. Dining out is now a form of stress-relief. Being convenient and very affordable can be seen by a busy parent as one less thing to do when they get home. Satisfying the needs of children is a powerful way to bring in families. McDonalds® created an empire by stimulating children's wants so parents will respond by dropping in.

6. Although, more people than ever eat away from home, pleasure is still a primary reason people dine out. Dining out is a way to reward yourself and others. The pleasure of dressing up for a special occasion or meeting friends for appetizers and a beer is a powerful motivator.

7. Attention (vanity) is a major influence on purchasing decisions, from shoes to homes. People need to feel good about themselves, and making them feel pampered is a great way to do just that. Another factor is the bolstering of social stature—the see-and-be-seen

factor. Dining out also gives people a way to show off to others.

8. Fellowship offers patrons another reason to visit your restaurant. Social gatherings at restaurants are a great way to connect. Think about providing diners with an atmosphere that they want to gather in, celebrate special occasions and mark important life events. A friendly environment and staff gives road-weary business travelers and lonely customers a chance to connect with other human beings.

9. Fear doesn't drive people to eat out but it does factor into their restaurant choices. Fear (and its cousin concern) manifests itself with patrons making food choices because of the health factor. Providing a solution that frees them from fear is a great way to tap into this emotional need. Whether you promote organic ingredients or low-fat menu items, you are providing them with one less thing to be fearful about.

Your Niche

What sets your restaurant apart can also be a strong way to capture your fair share of the market. Uniqueness is a great value to explore and include under your plan's competition section. Describe what makes you special. Do you have a food specialty or an entertainment factor that brings in people? Sometimes what sets you apart from your competition are mundane things like longer hours, free parking or kids-eat-free specials.

Look for ways to set your restaurant apart from the competition beyond overused descriptions like better food or friendlier service. People tend to tune these out.

Your Pricing

Setting appropriate prices requires a combination of financial analysis, competitive research and demographic data. So how much should you charge? Will your customers be able to afford $10 gourmet hamburgers with flavored mustards and hand-cut pomes frits or prefer low-cost fast-food burgers with extra relish?

At this stage, you most likely have not finalized your actual food costs, and overhead figures are still an estimate. There are factors that you can use to create pricing scenarios and compare these with competitors. The National Restaurant Association publishes an industry book on these annually revised ratios.

Your Brand

The process of creating a recognition factor for your business is called branding. Branding your restaurant starts with finding a name that connects with customers. The name might be something very chic like "Noir" or homey like "Mama Rosa's" or clever like "One Potato, Two Potato" or fun like "Mr. Mouse's House." The name you select should reflect the overall image you are trying to create.

If your legal name is different than your restaurant name, you'll need to file an assumed business name (also know as a "DBA" or "doing business as") with your local governing authority. Check with your city, county and state agencies governing new businesses and comply with their specific requirements. In addition, you may want to register the name and logo as trademarks. The U.S. Trademark and Patent Office has information available at **www.uspto.gov**. Check out the article on small-business trademarks at ABC Small Biz at **www.abcsmallbiz.com/bizbasics/gettingstarted/trademark.html**.

Along with your restaurant brand name, you'll need a logo and color scheme. Starting off with these will help you create a consistent message and appearance. Consistency is important in the branding process. A green logo here and orange logo elsewhere doesn't create a single image that you want people to think of when they think of your restaurant. Think of the golden arches of McDonalds® or the bright Coca-Cola® red that has never changed over the decades. An inconsistent image is one of the most common mistakes a new business makes.

Your Outreach

Advertising and PR are critical to attracting customers. How will you let your potential customers know about your restaurant? What types of paid advertising will you be implementing and what results do you expect? How and by whom will PR be handled?

Your advertising needs (and budget) are affected by your competitors' activities, your location and your local customers. Advertising has two primary functions. The first is to bring paying customers in; the second is to develop a brand name for your restaurant for long-term sales.

Bringing people in now should be your #1 goal with all advertising and public relations campaigns. In your early days, you'll need to keep the cash flow consistent to keep on top of expenses. However, you'll also need to commit, from day one, a percentage of your advertising budget to long-term brand building.

Your initial advertising efforts should concentrate on reaching potential customers within your neighborhood. Start by putting up a sign announcing your arrival the day you sign the lease or break ground. Start the buzz early with the media. Plan a community-wide grand opening (don't forget to invite suppliers and others who helped you launch your restaurant) and advertise it at least two weeks in advance.

To write your marketing section and establish a preliminary budget, you'll need to explore the various types of advertising and public relations efforts available in your community. From billboards to Web sites, there are dozens of ways to tell your story and bring in customers.

One of the most critical parts of developing ongoing advertising campaigns is your ability to measure its success. When people make reservations, ask how they heard about you. Leave a comment card at the table along with the check. Build in measurable response mechanisms such as coupons or frequent-buyer card programs.

The most effective advertising is the one that most frequently reaches your desired target audience. If your target audience is high school and college students, don't advertise in the local business journal. If your restaurant is a perfect business lunch spot, place an appropriate ad in that same journal.

Remember that advertising is an investment that can take some time to reap dividends. Create campaigns in multiple venues that will be repeatedly seen by prospective customers. Don't abandon ship if nothing seems to be happening the first week; advertising gurus advise patience, as it can take up to seven viewings before someone takes action.

Speaking of taking action: Don't be passive in your advertising. Be a little bossy! Tell people what you want them to do. Stop by and try our juicy cheeseburgers with hand-cut fries. Call today and make a reservation.

The best advertising is the great things people say about your restaurant. Word-of-mouth advertising will develop naturally but it is a slow process. You can rev that up by building in ways to promote loyalty, encourage people to refer you, and spend as much money on keeping your customers as you do on acquiring new ones!

Restaurant reviews are also word-of-mouth advertising. Reviewers like to visit the new spot in town. Do some dry runs and pre-opening events to get your kitchen and staff up to speed before a reviewer can drop by during your disorganized, we're-still-learning stage! Once someone hears a bad review, it can be difficult to overcome the memory.

Developing Your Advertising

Your plan readers will be interested in how you intend to advertise and how much you will spend doing it. If you aren't experienced in purchasing advertising, you'll need to do a bit of homework to learn the lingo and discuss the best venues for your restaurant's message. Remember, ad salespeople are just that: salespeople! While they are there to help you, they are also there to close deals, so be wary of the advice they give you.

When you think about advertising, you must consider where your ideal customer would most likely hear about you. Match your advertising to their habits. Concentrate on advertising methods that are closest to where your customers live and work. Sure, a huge freeway billboard is a real eye-catcher, but will it bring business to your restaurant 15 miles north?

To learn more about small business advertising, check out Jay Conrad Levinson at **www.gmarketing.com**. His advice and practical guerilla marketing philosophy are aimed at small businesses interested in maximizing their marketing efforts without breaking their budgets. He has authored several books on practical and affordable public relations and advertising.

Additional resources on small business advertising can be found in *Chapter 14 – Resources.*

Advertising Budgets

So how much should you spend on advertising? There is no right answer, as there are plenty of exceptions for every rule. However, as a new business that markets directly to consumers, your initial annual advertising budget will probably fall in the range of 10–15 percent of your anticipated revenues. If you don't have to compete with chain restaurants, you may find that 5–7 percent is sufficient, after you've successfully built a regular clientele.

Buying advertising means you can negotiate for the best deal. Here are a few ways to save advertising dollars:

- Ask if you can have a new customer test run.

- Check the cost difference between black and white and 4-color printing.

- Act as your own ad agency and ask for the 15 percent agency discount.

- Ask for multiple insertion discounts.

- Barter services if possible.

- Look for the best time slots when people are listening to radio or watching cable TV.

- Hire university students studying business and/or marketing.

When establishing your marketing (ads and PR) budgets, remember that advertising cycles can mean that you'll pay for an ad weeks before the magazine is on the newsstand. Look at your anticipated business cycles and keep your name in front of people in time to increase business during down periods. Don't wait until you're in a slump to start advertising.

It is possible to be a successful restaurateur without being an accounting wizard.

8

Financial Data

It is possible to be a successful restaurateur without being an accounting wizard. The key is to hire a good bookkeeper for daily tasks and an accountant for monthly, quarterly and annual financial reports and tax obligations. You can pay people to do the number crunching but you must know how to read and use the information in these reports. Your restaurant's accounting is not just something you do to please the IRS; it is your guide to your profitability.

In the financial section, you will be transforming your wish lists, budgets and assumptions into financial reports. A significant portion of your first projects will be conjecture based upon what you know at that time. The goal is to analyze and determine at what levels you will begin to become profitable, whether you have sufficient starting and working capital and whether your profit potential is worth your time and money investment.

During this process, you'll calculate how much money you need in addition to your personal investment. In order to qualify for a loan or investment, you must also be able to prove your ability to repay the loan or give an investor an appropriate return.

Hiring an accountant with food service operations experience can be a wise move. He or she will understand your business cycle, tax laws that apply to food service establishments, and be able to help you determine ways to improve your financial outlook.

Your Financial Management Plan

Sound financial management ensures your business will remain profitable and solvent. How well you manage your money is the cornerstone of every successful business venture. Each year apparently successful businesses fail because of poor or inadequate financial management. As a business owner, you will need to identify and implement policies and ensure that you can meet your financial obligations.

To effectively manage your finances, plan a sound, realistic budget by determining the actual amount of money needed to open your business (start-up costs) and the amount needed to keep it open (operating costs). The first step to building a sound financial plan is to devise a start-up budget. Your start-up budget will usually include such one-time-only costs as major equipment, utility deposits, down payments, etc.

The financial section of your business plan should include any loan applications you have filed, your capital equipment and supply list, balance sheet, break-even analysis, pro-forma income projections (profit and loss statement) and pro-forma cash flow. The income statement and cash flow projections should include a three-year summary (detail by month for the first year, then by quarter for the second and third years).

Developing projections is probably the most difficult aspect of writing your business plan. You should strive to be as accurate as possible based upon your research. Overstating your sales in hopes of impressing lenders or investors can backfire on you should you not reach these estimates. Understating your sales can mean that you won't be prepared to satisfy the demand.

The accounting system (including sales and inventory management) along with your fiscal calendar dates are addressed in this section of the business plan.

Starting-Out Needs

In *Chapter 14 – Resources*, you'll find a master list to work from. Your start-up capital must cover everything from your business license to telephone company deposits to stocking the freezer. Investigate these thoroughly as they can quickly add up.

You'll need to document your source(s) for your available cash along with discussing your assumptions on calculating specific estimated expenses. For example, food and beverage ingredients may require an approximation based upon your food service experience, as final pricing negotiations may take some time.

If your start-up costs don't exceed your available cash, you'll be explaining what the balance will be used for. If you are still seeking additional financing, you'll weigh this use against upcoming needs. If your start-up costs are greater than your available cash, you'll need to discuss where the balance will be coming from. This can be a combination of personal investment, loans or outside investment.

Operating Budget

An operating budget is prepared when you are actually ready to open for business. The operating budget will reflect your priorities in terms of how you spend your money, the expenses you will incur and how you will meet those expenses (income). Your operating budget will include additional investment or loans necessary to cover the first six to nine months of operation.

If a franchise, the franchiser may stipulate in the franchise contract the type of accounting and inventory systems you may use. If this is the case, he or she should have a system already intact and you will be required to adopt this system. Whether you develop the accounting and inventory systems yourself, have an outside financial advisor develop the systems, or the franchiser provides these systems, you will need to acquire a thorough understanding of each segment and how it operates. Your financial advisor can assist you in developing this section of your business plan.

The following questions should help you determine the amount of start-up capital you will need to purchase and open a franchise.

- How much money do you have?

- How much money will you need to purchase the franchise?

- How much money will you need for start-up?

- How much money will you need to stay in business?

Other questions that you will need to consider are:

- What are your sales and profit goals for the coming year?

- Will the franchiser establish your sales and profit goals? Will they expect you to reach and retain a certain sales level and profit margin?

- What financial projections will you need to include in your business plan?

- What kind of inventory-control system will you use?

Your plan should include an explanation of all projections. Unless you are thoroughly familiar with financial statements, get help in preparing your cash flow and income statements and your balance sheet. Your aim is not to become a financial wizard, but to understand the financial tools well enough to gain their benefits. Your accountant or financial advisor can help you accomplish this goal.

Loan Application

Your lender will supply you with the appropriate applications. These should be readable and completed accurately. If your handwriting isn't the best, find a typewriter or someone with better penmanship.

Capital Equipment and Supply List

Capital equipment is any equipment with a useful life of one year or more that is used in the creation and sale of a product or service. Typically, equipment is freestanding and can be resold. For example, a new glass display case is a capital equipment purchase while a new drive-up window is a real property improvement.

If you aren't building from the ground-up or undergoing an extensive building renovation, your biggest expense will be furnishings and equipment. Start with a master wish list and start plugging in your estimated costs for new and used equipment.

Think used: Unfortunately, the failure rate of restaurants is significant enough that there seems to be plenty of top-quality used equipment on the market at all times. Used equipment (especially for behind-the-scenes needs where looks aren't important) can be a wise investment.

Your supply list includes the consumables that you'll need to set up an office, your kitchen and your public areas. Consumables can be everything from toilet paper to flour (anything that is used up and requires restocking). Dinnerware is typically considered a consumable as pieces become broken and worn and replacement cycles are short.

Crunching More Numbers

Many businesspeople look glassy-eyed when they sit down to create the financial reports needed to document their cash flow and income projections. Computer software can make it much easier on you. Intuit's QuickBooks Premier offers a variety of tools to help you create these. PlanMagic Restaurant Plan (**www.planmagic.com**) includes 35 food service-specific financial spreadsheets. Virtual Restaurant (**www.virtualrestaurant.com /prices.htm**) also offers Excel 97 and above financial spreadsheet templates.

If accounting terms, ratios and financial calculations aren't a normal part of your businessperson's vocabulary, purchase a basic accounting book such as *Understanding Business Accounting for Dummies.* You must know and understand these terms.

To prepare your financial statements, you'll have to make some basic assumptions from which to build upon. Your plan should explain these. Assumptions are just educated guesses, such as you'll be turning tables three times per hour or that your average ticket size will be $24. To calculate sales, you need to look at things like counts and turns.

The National Restaurant Association offers a book on industry operations ratios and statistics from which you can draw assumptions for your restaurant. These assumptions will help you calculate your forward looking financial reports. Available to members at **www.restaurant.org/research/operations /overview.cfm**.

Financial consultants Hornung & Associates, LLC (**www.hornungllc.com/restaurant.htm**) sell the Restaurant Analyzer, an analytical tool based upon the same National Restaurant Association industry statistics.

Balance Sheet

A balance sheet is just that—a statement where all your assets are listed and weighed against all of your liabilities. Assets less your liabilities equals your net worth as of a specific date. Your accounting software can create this for you quickly and easily.

Break-Even Analysis

Break-even is where sales pay for the cost of doing business (your overhead) plus the cost of goods sold. Sales beyond this level are your profits. Sales in a restaurant are comprised of the number of customers you serve (covers) and the per-person spending (average check).

Break-even can also be expressed by the number of customers served, the number of times a table turns and other quantities. Below are a few types of analysis restaurant owners have found to be helpful.

- **Covers (customers served)** — Shows approximately how many customers you must serve (can be broken down by meal periods, days, weeks, months or quarters) to break even. You'll start by calculating an average sale per customer figure. Since the average meal cost varies from breakfast, lunch and dinner, separating these meal periods out will give you more accurate data. For example, breakfast might average $6.75 per person while dinner is $12.55. For new restaurants, you'll need to establish imaginary meals for imaginary customers.

By figuring out how many customers you need to break even, you'll be able to assess whether your facility and staff can actually handle the volume. You can then establish some profit-making and growth goals. The customers served in break-even data can also be helpful in determining whether a major purchase (such as an Italian espresso machine) or renovation (expanding the dining room by ten tables) will attract sufficient new customers to pay for itself in an acceptable period.

- **Turns** — Turns are the number of times a table is filled and refilled during a specific period. This period is typically a mealtime or a day. Calculating the number of turns required to break even during a meal period will demonstrate whether you will be able to seat and serve enough customers to cover all meal and overhead costs and make a profit.

In the following scenario, it takes 2.45 turns to break even—everything above that becomes profit.

Let's assume that during the noon hour...	Per Table	# of Tables	For 1 Turn per Table
Average ticket (all parties at one table)	$24.00	22	$528.00 (total sales)
Food costs per table	$11.50	22	$253.00 (food costs)
Gross profit per table (ticket less food cost)	$12.50	22	$275.00 (gross profit)
Overhead (operational costs plus personnel costs)		$674.00 (overhead for all tables)	2.45 turns (minimum to cover overhead $674 divided by $275)

Income Projections

Your income projections serve as a model for profitability and to benchmark your progress. If you have an existing restaurant, you'll provide actual profit and loss statements and provide some income projections based upon historical data and known upcoming activities, flavored with your vision of the future. New restaurants won't have any history (although, if you are purchasing an existing business or investing in a franchise, you may have some data to use as a baseline) so you'll be taking what you do know and creating some probable scenarios to project your anticipated income and expenses for your first year, year three and year five.

Some projections will be based upon assumptions that are nothing more than educated guesses. In this financial data section, you'll establish and define the important assumptions. Assumptions such as families will still want to eat great pizza are a given. You'll be explaining that participating in a local farmers' market will bring in five new customers a week or your average ticket will be $29.95 for food and beverages.

Your profit and loss projections will need to be created for the upcoming three years. For your first year of a new restaurant, you'll need month-by-month statements. All businesses have sales cycles based upon the seasons, community events and the days of the week. Your month-by-month breakdown should take into account all anticipated external events that will positively or negatively affect your sales. This first-year look is your benchmark period. You'll be able to compare your pro-forma projections with your actual sales. This is a learning process that will help you review and update your assumptions and projections.

The second and third years will need profit and loss statements by quarters with a summary at the end of each year. The last income projection report will be a summary report that includes all three years.

Pro-Forma Cash Flow

Pro-forma refers to a financial document prepared in advance to use as a basis for decision-making or fiscal activities. Incoming cash flow is the money that comes in from sales, investors, loans or sale of assets. Outgoing cash flow are the payments and cash expenditures you make to pay suppliers, employees, long-term debts and taxes. Pro-forma cash flow reports document when these should transactions occur.

Insufficient or inconsistent incoming cash can cripple a business. Understanding and monitoring your cash flow may actually be a better predictor of your financial success than a profit and loss statement. You can actually be profitable on paper, but if the cash isn't there when the bills are due, you are in financial distress.

Net cash flow is the difference between incoming cash and outgoing cash. Start-up costs and unforeseen expenses during your launch can quickly gobble up your cash. Preparing cash flow reports will help you discover periods where working capital can keep your bills paid on time and paychecks funded.

Planware at **www.planware.org** has a variety of software financial projection planners including various cash flow planning tools for U.S., Canadian and U.K. users.

9

Researching Your Business Concept

Researching Your Market and Competition

Your market is the potential customers who are or could be convinced to purchase food products similar to your restaurant offerings. This includes a geographical territory of potential customers and competitors vying for the same dining dollar.

Market and competition research will be the most time-consuming and valuable information you'll need to gather and analyze. Being diligent and thorough can prevent you from making costly mistakes. You'll be looking at a broad range of issues and how they support (or perhaps even disprove) your restaurant/business concept and profit potential.

Let's start with an idea and explore various ways you might research the viability of this idea. Let's say you want to open a small café on the first floor of a busy office building. Your first step will be to research potential locations. Your café will primarily serve the people who work in the building so researching all the cafés around the city won't provide you with the targeted information you need. You need to know about the customers and competitors within a short walking distance.

Location, Location, Location

Where your restaurant lives can make or break it! If you are writing a plan for a new restaurant venture, you may be interested in buying land and building. (In *Chapter 6 – Feasibility Studies,* I talk about studying and analyzing your location.) You can look at a location based upon an entire community, a neighborhood, a specific land parcel, traffic flow, the health of a mall or construction costs.

Location = Customers

In starting a new restaurant, the most important consideration for locating your restaurant is where your customers are. If you have to spend a little more or sacrifice a need to be better situated for your customers, it probably is worth it. If you first address your customer needs, you'll have a better financial basis to make your location work for you and your staff.

Consider these questions when addressing this section of your business plan:

1. What are your location needs?

2. What kind of space will you need? Is there room to expand?

3. Are there environmental or zoning issues to be considered?

4. Why is the area desirable? The building desirable?

5. Is it easily accessible? Is public transportation available? Is street lighting adequate?

6. Is it affordable?

Building Your Own

Building your own restaurant takes time and significant capital. From looking at property through drawing up architectural plans to obtaining zoning variances and building permits to opening the front door can take as long as two years—and perhaps even longer.

Although you'll be hiring experts to handle the project, you will need to be intimately involved in every stage. There are plenty of ways for a major construction project to go off track, costing you time and money.

To learn about building your own restaurant from scratch, I'd suggest you read *The Food Service Professionals Guide to Restaurant Design: Designing, Constructing & Renovating a Food Service Establishment* by Atlantic Publishing and *Restaurant Site Location: Finding Negotiating & Securing The Best Food Service Site for Maximum Profit* by Atlantic Publishing.

These books cover in-depth topics such as:

- The essential characteristics of the best location.

- Increasing your profits by choosing the right location.

- Dealing with zoning ordinances, parking availability, transportation facilities and natural barriers (freeways, hills and bridges), environmental impact, accessibility and visibility of your restaurant.

- Hiring and working with architects, planners, developers, builders and decorators.

- How to protect yourself from construction-related legal issues.

Buying an Existing Business

Purchasing an existing business can be the fastest way to get your doors open; however, it may not be the best choice for success. Remember, if the location is a poor one, the prior business had a bad reputation, or the equipment is overpriced, you may be hindering your potential. Availability is another factor when purchasing an existing business; the right business for you has to be on the market now or you have to make an offer that they cannot refuse.

Business brokers help buyers and sellers connect (just as a real estate broker does). Start by finding a business broker who will represent you and your interests. He or she will be able to research cafés for sale in office buildings within your desired geographical area. Depending upon your level of urgency, it might take months or even a year to find the right spot for your café. Your broker may even approach business owners on your behalf to explore buying them out. Look for operations where a long-term lease can be assumed by a new owner.

To learn more about buying an existing restaurant business, check out *Buying, Selling & Leasing A Restaurant For Maximum Profit: 365 Secrets Revealed* by Lynda Andrews (Atlantic Publishing).

Buying Costs

Buyers must estimate, as accurately as possible, the total initial investment needed to get their businesses up and running the way they envision them. Many restaurants that could have been successful failed because they were undercapitalized. For exactly this reason, one of the very appealing aspects of purchasing an existing restaurant is that many start-up costs are avoided. There are, however, a number of start-up costs even with transfer of ownership. Here are a number to be aware of:

- **Investigation costs** — Be willing to spend time and money to thoroughly examine the opportunities that are available. Many investors falsely believe that once initial development work is complete, the start-up costs are eliminated. These costs still exist and wise investors calculate them in their analyses.

- **Down payment** — A standard down payment is usually around a quarter of the sales price. The down payment can affect the sales price, and in many cases sellers will accept a lower sales price with a larger down payment and vice versa.

- **Transaction costs** — Prorated insurance, payroll, property taxes, vacation pay, license renewal fees, advertising costs, etc., on the close-of-escrow date.

- **Working capital** — Available cash to ensure sufficient supplies are on hand to run the restaurant.

- **Deposits** — Cash deposits required of the new owner for utility, telephone, sales tax, payroll-tax and lease deposits.

- **Licenses and permits** — All required operating licenses and permits for retail, health and occupational

- **Legal fees** — Fees for legal advice, buyer negotiation and contract review.

- **Renovations** — Costs required to renovate or rectify building code violations.

- **Equipment and utensils** — Costs to purchase new or replacement equipment, supplies and serving ware. Don't forget to include maintenance agreements.

- **Advertising**—Costs to promote an opening or reopening, rebuild signage and offer promotional discounts and incentives.

- **Fictitious name registration**—Also know as "doing business as" or "DBA." If the name of a restaurant doesn't use your own name, the name usually must be registered at the local courthouse or County Recorder's Office.

- **Loan fees**—Loan fees from the lending parties.

- **Equity fees**—Attorney, document preparation and registration fees for selling common stock.

- **Insurance**—Lender-required life and disability insurance with the lender named as sole beneficiary. Adequate real property insurance may also be required.

- **Franchise**—Franchise transfer-of-ownership fee. This fee pays the franchiser for the costs of evaluating the new owner for the franchise. It is paid up-front and in cash before the new franchise can begin operations.

- **Distributorship fees**—Exclusive distributorship licenses or discontinuing a current license agreement may incur costs similar to franchise fees.

- **Pre-opening labor**—Labor required during the pre-opening and transition period.

- **Accounting fees**—Fees for assistance in the evaluation of a restaurant purchase.

- **Other consulting fees**—Fees for specialty services such as consultants, labor-relations specialists and computer consultants.

- **Other prepaid expenses**—Any prepayment required by a creditor.

- **Sales taxes**—Property subject to a transfer tax and non-food supplies are often subject to sales tax.

- **Locksmith**—Cost to change all the locks on a business after the sale is concluded.

- **Security**—Transfer or set-up fee for security service or systems.

- **Contingency**—A contingency fund large enough for at least the first six months' operating expenses. Among other things, it is often necessary to over-hire and over-schedule employees before an effective sales distribution pattern emerges, so operators incur incredibly high expenses during the first six months of operation. Not having an ample contingency fund is the primary reason many businesses fail within the first few months.

Leasing Space

Commercial realtors typically handle office space leasing even in new construction projects. Retrofitting a space for food service can be costly, so people often look for empty spaces that formerly held a food-oriented business. There are some caveats that might become obstacles such as poor word-of-mouth and the failed-location syndrome. Experienced restaurateurs know that opening an establishment where a restaurant has already failed increases your chances for failing also. This myth seems to hold true time and time again. Restaurants don't fail because they are busy and enjoyed by customers; they fail for common reasons that can also adversely affect your business.

Your commercial realtor can help you negotiate favorable lease terms along with renovation allowances and other incentives.

Here are some tips if you are currently leasing space and want to move on:

- Check your current lease before you begin searching for a new one. You want to time your new lease to coincide with your current lease ending unless you have a no-penalty exit clause. Start your new location search several months in advance as a better location may be hard to find. Also be careful about giving your lessor too much advanced notice of a pending move as this can work against you.

- Check out subletting options. If your current lease gives you the option to sublet the property, you might actually turn a profit on subletting. This profit can be used to offset the cost of a newer, larger or better restaurant location. Have your attorney review your lease to determine your legal rights.

- Ask about a buyout. If you cannot or do not want to sublet the property and must leave before your current lease expires, ask your lessor about the possibility of a buyout. This is a negotiated or set amount of money that the leaseholder will accept to let you out of your lease agreement. This may be less than what you would pay over the balance of your lease.

Geographically-Based Research

Once you have selected two or three potential locations for your café, you can begin to research your potential customer base and competitors. The building's leasing agent can provide you with general information about tenants along with the number of people who work in the building.

When developing a food service business within another business (within a mall or within an office building), you will be connecting your future with the economic health of the tenants. Being in a building that houses 500 people who are about to be laid off can be unwise for you. Once you know a bit about the companies who operate within the building, spend some time doing some background research. Research each business as if you were going to be an investor (which, in a way, you will be).

Check your local newspaper's business section archives (many are now online) for articles, consult with your stock broker on investment potential, and search online through sites such as Hoovers (**www.hoovers.com**) and The Motley Fool (**www.fool.com**).

Observation Techniques

Some low-tech observation methods can provide you with excellent demographic data. The leasing agent can assist you with notifying the building's security team of your presence and purpose for hanging around. With pad and paper in hand, spend time in the lobby observing passers-by.

Your assumption: You will be open at Monday through Friday at 7:30 a.m. Arrive early enough to catch the early birds in this busy building. Count and observe people as they arrive. How many are carrying food bags and cups?

Ask Questions

Poll office workers in public areas, nearby parks and (with the permission of their employers) with handouts. You might have prepaid postcards printed with a few questions that you hand out. Offer a contest incentive such as theater tickets or a dinner for two to increase participation. Ask questions such as, "How often do you leave the building for lunch?" "What's your favorite quick, nearby lunch spot?"

How Will I Know If I'm on the Right Track?

If you've never been in a management capacity in the food service or hospitality industries, you probably don't have points of reference on which to judge whether your plan is fiscally sound, if your numbers are realistic or if your assumptions are valid.

Plenty of people in the restaurant industry are asking the same questions and getting answers from experts and peers with no strings attached. A good place to start is with your state restaurant association and the various national trade associations. There are also plenty of peer-to-peer online forums where you can ask questions and run ideas past others. The community spirit of the Web can prove to be an invaluable tool. Check *Chapter 14 – Resources* for food service/hospitality industry support groups.

It has probably been years since you've written a term paper. This chapter will help refresh your memory on creative data gathering methods and research techniques. Your goal is to have all the information you need to prove your thesis.

In writing a business plan, your thesis isn't a complex theoretical statement. A simple thought sums it up — "My idea for a [insert your concept here] restaurant is a profitable one." Your research goal is to prove this statement accurate. If you cannot, you need to rethink your idea and revise it.

Getting Organized

Creating a data-gathering and filing system from the get-go will save you time and headaches along the way and make the writing process easier. To follow are some practical tips to get you started. Whatever system you set up won't work unless you feel comfortable about using it and you make it a habit! It takes just a few minutes to minimize panic during late night writing sessions.

While you are actively exploring your restaurant dream, you'll find that ideas pop into your head while driving, just before you drop off to sleep and other unusual times. That's why you need a way to conveniently jot down these ideas. Check out the micro recorders at your local office supply or electronic store. You can carry these with you at all times and they'll even tuck into your pajama pocket!

- Never leave home without:

    ○ Notepad and pen (or your micro recorder)—all ideas have merit so don't censor yourself. Write your reminders here and follow-up at the end of the day.

    ○ Business cards—make it easy for people to get back to you with requested information.

    ○ Expandable travel folder—information comes in all sizes and shapes so just drop it in to sort out at the end of the day.

- Set up a business plan file cabinet.

    ○ This can be a drawer in an existing file cabinet or a self-contained plastic version.

- Create hanging files and file folders. Divide info into categories. Your categories can follow a business plan outline or be of your own creation.

- Empty your mind, pockets and travel folder daily.

  - By taking just a few minutes to review, sort and file data gathered that day, you'll also be able to make notes and comments that may be lost to you weeks from now.

- Create a contact list. Whether this is a small address book or electronic personal digital assistant, start gathering and carrying your contact list.

  - Don't forget to ask for a business card when you meet people.

  - Make notes so you'll remember how and why this person can be helpful.

  - Get e-mail addresses and Web sites.

  - Cross-index referrals. If Norman Taylor refers you to Betty Donaldson, make a note so you can name drop like this: "Hello, my name is [your name]. I'm doing research for a new business I am launching and Norman Taylor of Taylor Accounting referred me to you as someone who might help me."

- Buy and send thank-you notes.

  - Your local stationery or office supply store will have professional-looking generic thank-you notes. Drop one in the mail when someone goes out of his or her way to provide assistance. This polite act is a great way to start a buzz within your community about your new restaurant.

- Create a master to-do/reminder/follow-up list.

  - At the end of the day, transfer your notes and audio memos to a master list. Don't wait too long or you'll forget what your scribbling means!

    ◊ Not every question can be answered in one phone call or visit, so a follow-up list will keep you from forgetting something.

    ◊ Research tends to turn up other research possibilities. Add these on your master to-do list.

- Create a Business Plan favorite (bookmark) folder and e-mail inbox.

  - An enormous amount of research information is available on the Web. Create subtopic folders so you can categorize and find bookmarked sites quickly.

    ◊ A great organizational tool for Web research is Onfolio at **www.onfolio.com**. You can flag by importance, write reminder descriptions, search

> your notes by keyword and even save text from a site and file it.

- ○ If you are sending out e-mails requesting information, sort your outgoing messages and incoming responses into a "Business Plan" inbox folder. Check your e-mail client software for ways to make this automatic and to flag activity for you.

Create a Research List

Your research list consists of questions that you don't know the answers to right now. The answers should prove:

1. There is a need for your restaurant.

2. There are ample paying customers available to you.

3. You can be competitive in pricing, service and food quality.

4. Your location works for you and your future customers.

5. You can make it happen.

Write down all the questions your partners, lawyer, lender, investors, accountant, management team, creative personnel and family might ask about your new or expanding restaurant.

To get you started, here are some typical types of questions to which you'll need answers:

1. Is your desired location zoned for commercial activities?

2. Will people want you to be open for breakfast?

3. Do you need to build your own facility or can you find appropriate space to lease?

4. Are your food offerings too trendy? too late in the trend cycle?

5. Will you have enough potential patrons who enjoy your ethnic cuisine?

6. How much will you have to spend to outfit your kitchen?

7. Will you need to register your name as a trademark or service mark?

8. Will you be able to obtain a liquor license?

9. Are there environmental rules or other laws that will prohibit you from using a piece of equipment or hanging a sign?

10. Can your meals be competitively priced and profitable?

Assumptions Are Not Conclusions

When deciding what data you need to construct your business plan, don't make unnecessary assumptions. Assumptions, by definition, are personal beliefs not supported by fact. Assuming you'll be able to get a needed code variance or your town needs another pizza parlor can be costly errors in judgment.

Assumptions aren't a reliable foundation for decision-making and business success. If you believe something to be true—prove it! Unsupported claims may make your plan look strong but they do everyone a disservice.

Conclusions are not assumptions. After researching your new restaurant plan, you will be drawing some conclusions. These conclusions aren't going to be 100 percent accurate (unless you can read a crystal ball). However if they are fact-based and reasonable, they will be what convinces your banker to lend you money and investors to write that check.

Types of Research

There are two basic types of research you can conduct on your own. The first is primary research where you speak directly with people about their opinions and the second is secondary research where you are researching information previously gathered by others, and interpreting it to prove something.

Primary Research

The types of primary research you would typically be conducting are through observation and questioning. Primary research is intimate, local and typically inexpensive to gather. Review your research questions and see which might be answered by observing people or things and questioning potential or current customers, government officials, industry experts and business peers.

Things that you might observe are the numbers of cars that pass by your intended restaurant location from 5:30 a.m. to 9 a.m. or the family size and ages of a competitors' drive-through window at dinner hour. Visit competitors during various days and times to observe wait times, customer overflow and other areas you might improve upon. While not necessarily scientific, this type of data gathering can prove to be invaluable.

As an example, let's assume you are preparing to open a pancake house and want information on traffic volume and flow past your store. If you are going to refer to your observations in your business plan, you'll need to:

- **Be as accurate as you can.** With pad in hand, keep careful count and thorough notes.

- **Take an ample sample size.** Don't just sit there on a Sunday morning before church and assume this data will be accurate. Count cars Monday through Sunday for several weeks and create daily and weekly averages. Perhaps you'll discover that the Sunday traffic after church could be more important to you or that the best day of the week to be closed is Tuesday.

- **Observe other traffic draws.** Are there office buildings or stores nearby that would bring potential patrons to your location?

    Observe traffic flow. Is it difficult for people to turn into your location? Is the traffic moving by too swiftly to notice your sign?

Questioning. Asking questions can mean anything from passing out a questionnaire to existing customers, asking government employees pertinent questions and opinions, taking a street-side poll, or conducting a telephone survey.

Using our pancake house scenario, here are some research questions you might consider. Use these as stimulus for information you might gather using this method.

- **Is the new overpass going to redirect traffic flow?** Your city or county planning commission or state Department of Transportation can advise you of future road projects that could affect your business.

- **What's the future of other new businesses located nearby?** Multi-family developments or single-family home projects? Your local planning commissions, zoning boards, economic development agencies and chamber of commerce can tell you about pending changes. Landholders, leasing agents and real estate agents can provide you with rumors that may warrant research. Besides looking for growth to support your business, look for negative situations that can create economic stress on your community, impact dining trends in your service area, etc.

- **How often do you eat breakfast away from home each week?** Drive-through service or sit-down? School or office setting? You might hand out postage-paid survey cards to potential customers in the community. Try a door-to-door campaign. Stand on a nearby street corner and ask passers-by. Telemarketing was once a common gathering tool; however, privacy regulations have virtually eliminated this method. Send bulk mail letters (see the U.S.P.S. for carrier route bulk mail programs), asking for your neighbor's help might even work.

Secondary Research

We are in the age of information so there is very little that someone hasn't tallied already. Every level of American government is consumed with gathering data. There are also thousands of companies (profit-oriented and non-profit) that count, ask, and add up what we like, where we live, who we are, why we buy, what we earn, and so forth.

In determining your potential for profitability, you will need to look carefully at industry statistics, economic trends and demographic information. The food service/restaurant/ hospitality industry gathers statistics regularly. See *Chapter 14 –*

Resources for some organizations that may have what you are looking for. They will also have informative articles on economic and food trends that can affect your restaurant. The U.S. government also keeps track of restaurant industry statistics in broader terms. The U.S. government Web portal, First Gov, has information at **www.firstgov.gov/Business/ Industry_Tourism .html**. The IRS (**www.irs.gov**), Bureau of Labor Statistics (**www.bls.gov**), U.S. Census Bureau (**www.census.gov**) and Federal Stats (**www.fedstats.gov**) offer plenty of numbers for your use. Look for the most current reports.

Economic information is the financial health of your community and the overall U.S. economy as a predictor of buying power, spending habits and economic predictors that help or hurt small businesses. Restaurants are immediately affected by economic up- and downturns. Although food is a necessity and dining out frequency continues to rise, dining out is still considered a discretionary expense that can be cut or eliminated based upon personal financial situations.

Demographic information reports on human populations. Restaurant owners use demographic information that details their community and isolates their ideal customer and their habits. (See *Chapter 6* on your ideal customer and gathering information on them.) The types of demographic information that you'll find useful are numbers, marital status, family sizes, average household income, educational background, career information. This information will help you determine if there are ample potential customers from which to draw, if your food will appeal to these people, if they can afford your menu pricing, and if they dine out often in your style of restaurant.

The demographics suitable for family oriented buffet are quite different from a traditional French dinner house. Knowing what your ideal customer looks like and whether there enough of them in your neighborhood are critical.

Ask for Help

Sometimes finding an answer can be difficult to locate. However, one of the most powerful research tools is readily available to you at no cost—simply ask for help. Ask politely and give people ample time to respond and you'll be surprised at what you can learn. The help you receive can also come in the form of opinions, recommendations and referrals to other resources.

Ask:

- **Family and friends.** Their opinions (even biased ones) may lead in you a specific direction.

- **Peers.** Recommendations can save you time and money.

- **Trade and business organizations.** The National Restaurant Association, local and national chambers of commerce, local and national Better Business Bureau and SCORE are just a few organizations designed to support small business. You'll find a list of resources in *Chapter 14.*

- **Government agencies.** City, county, state and federal governmental bodies are the largest gatherers of information, and all of it is free. Finding the person who holds the key to the data can be worth all that time standing in line or waiting on hold. Don't forget the Web, as information and records are now being transferred to online databases.

- **Educational sources.** Colleges and universities along with non-profit foundations aimed at supporting small business endeavors can be very helpful.

- **Customers.** Take a survey of passers-by or ask current customers their opinion.

- **Competitors.** Not all competitors are wary of your inquiries, but remember that it is rude to ask confidential information. A nice chat with a waiter or bartender may give you the answer you need. Other information may be a matter of public record. Check with the appropriate government agency. Check private organizations such as Dun & Bradstreet (**www.smallbusiness.dnb.com**) and Hoovers Online (**www.hoovers.com**) for background information. Publicly held companies (chain restaurants and franchises) are required to file financial reports for investors. You'll find a wealth of information on these entities online including business gossip.

- **Local businesses.** Locate a networking group of local businesses or other entrepreneur clubs.

The Art of Asking for Research Help

Your attitude, preparedness and sincerity will go a long way in getting the help you need. The busy clerk behind the counter will probably go the extra mile for you and may even share something extra.

1. **Be gracious and ask politely**. The Bible says the "meek shall inherit the earth"; they will also have better luck getting the information they need.

2. **Allow ample time.** Don't arrive five minutes before closing time and expect someone to dig through dusty archives. You might even call ahead to learn the best times to drop by, schedule an appointment or reserve a research room.

3. **Know what you need.** You may not know exactly what you want, but if you can explain the question for which you are trying to find an answer, you'll have a better chance of finding the right answer.

4. **Be prepared.** Some services may require copy or other service fees. Have ample cash. Again, you might call ahead and ask if there are any fees. Bring along pen and paper.

5. **Plan ahead.** Don't wait until the last minute to ask for research help. Some records may be archived and require someone to take extra time to locate them.

6. **Say thank you.** These powerful words curry favors so use them liberally.

Hiring Research Help

If the only free time you have to research your book is after normal business hours, you'll be depending primarily upon Web resources. Another option is to hire someone to assist you with your research. A professional researcher will have a bag full of resources from which to draw. To locate a local researcher, use a search engine with the keyword "researcher" and your city name or contact your local library or college for a referral. University business departments may be able to connect you with a grad student interested in handling your research needs. Professional market research firms such as Market Research (**www.marketresearch.com**) and or BizVida (**www.bizvida.com**) can assist with a wide variety of research topics.

Hire a Financial Expert

Working with a certified public accountant (CPA) is probably worth every cent you'll pay. Even the most seasoned businessperson could use some hands-on number crunching and advice when it comes to financial projects that span five years or more. Paying someone to create these necessary financial reports for your plan is certainly fine; however, the most important aspect is to understand them and be able to easily analyze each.

If you are a new entrepreneur, make a wise investment in a couple of hours of one-on-one time with your CPA to learn accounting terms, how to read and interpret standard business reports (profit and loss, balance sheet and various accounting formulas/ratios) and intermediate financial decision-making skills.

If you want to go it alone, think about taking a business-owner class (locally or online) on understanding financial statements. Your local library or bookstore will also have books such as *Accounting for Dummies* by John A. Tracy and *Financial Statements for Non-Financial People: A Quick-And-Easy Guide to Reading a Financial Statement* by Ron Price. For restaurant-specific accounting information, visit Atlantic Publishing at **www.atlantic-pub.com**.

A good place to start your plan is to sort out your research and support materials into basic categories that coordinate with a standard business plan format.

10

Writing Your Plan

After days, weeks and perhaps even months of research and accounting, it is time to put it all down on paper. Your 20-minute elevator pitch (discussed in the *Introduction*) was your first writing assignment, so with that description in mind and your completed research, you are ready to start your full business plan.

Gather Your Data

A good place to start is to sort out your research and support materials into basic categories that coordinate with a standard business plan format (see *Chapter 5*). Information may actually be used in more than one section, but file it into the most logical category. Create a file folder or pocket folder for each category.

Next go through each folder and organize your data based upon its potential value to your writing. Highlight important information and attach your notes and reminders to the related research materials. This will help you find what you need, when you need it.

Now is the time to create a list of any information that appears to be missing. You'll have this list to refer to when you revisit bookmarked Web sites, reread articles, and sort through your scribbled notes during the writing process.

"Blank Screen, Go Away"

Writing doesn't come easy for many people. The blank piece of paper or computer monitor staring at you doesn't help. Even professional writers sometimes have difficulty getting started. Here are a few tips:

1. **Start with the easiest parts first.** Just because there is a standardized business plan format, doesn't mean you can't work on sections in any order you like!

2. **Try writing in longhand.** Just the act of changing to a different medium can sometimes help. Not everyone feels comfortable at the keyboard. You can even write the entire document by hand and have a typist or consultant format everything for publication.

3. **Write in a natural voice.** Although the language of business can be stiff and formal, don't let this become an obstacle. You can always go back and make it sound professional after you express your ideas and provide convincing arguments. Again, a business plan writer/consultant can actually take this and fashion a formal business plan.

4. **Write what pops into your head.** Often we tend to over-think what we want to say when the first idea is often the best one. Get it written down and then think

about how you can edit or improve it. Ideas cannot vanish into thin air once they are written down.

Coping with Writer Anxiety

Sometimes writer's block (where you cannot seem to get words on paper) turns into writer's anxiety. Purdue University offers some great tips on coping with the natural anxiety people feel when writing a boring, yet important paper at **http://owl.english .purdue.edu/handouts/general/gl_anxiety.html**.

Writing Formally

1. **Remove all the extra words.** A common mistake in business writing in a more formal tone is to add unnecessary words. See, I just didn't need those descriptive words to tell you what I meant. If in doubt, leave it out, and read the sentence aloud. If thought is clear, you don't need it.

2. **Set your spell/grammar checker to formal.** Some spell checkers allow you to set the document style for word usage and grammar to formal styles where, for example, contractions are not used.

Using an Outline Format

Automated outline formats are standard in word processing programs. Your user manual or interactive help system can guide you on how to use this formatting tool. (See how I have written the business plan contents in outline form in *Chapter 5*.)

The Most Important Advice

1. **Don't carry around all your notes, statistics and research.** Even if you think you'll have time during a lunch break to work on your plan, your research and notes could be easily damaged or lost. If you must work away from your office or home, take copies of critical information and keep the originals in tact. That way you can scribble fleeting ideas on them!

2. **Back up your work!** Do not live dangerously. Why risk your hard work when it only takes a few minutes to create a backup? There are automated backup programs, online backup services and even the basic floppy disk backup. Just be certain to back up all accounting, spreadsheets and written documents after each work session.

11

Getting Your Plan "Published"

Your business plan (whether you or someone else writes it) will need to be published. How you present your research, analysis and business ideas play an important part in impressing lenders, investors and others. A professional presentation tells people you are serious. In earlier chapters, we focused on gathering, writing, and formatting your ideas and plan. In this chapter, we'll explain how to put everything together in a single package.

If you've used a word processor and written each section in a different file, combine the files in the proper order to create a master file. You can either copy or paste or use the insert file function. Once you have created a master business plan document, you'll follow each step below in the order listed.

1. **Spell-check the entire document.** Using your word processor's built-in spelling, syntax and grammar checker will help you catch some (but never all) common mistakes. Never rely on their accuracy. Not only do they have problems with sound-like words,

they often get confused with more complex sentence structures. A dictionary, Thesaurus and a grammar book should be your guides. You can also hire a professional to edit your document.

2. **Read the entire document aloud.** This will help you hear areas that might confuse your target reader and catch grammar errors. Beware: You may not be able to trust your ability to hear problems, as proofing and reviewing your own writing can be difficult. Since you know what it is suppose to say, it is easy for your mind to not see what is actually written. You might have a spouse or friend read for you so you can concentrate on listening to every word. Remember that your document will have a more formal tone than your normal speaking style so don't get hung up on that.

3. **Review facts and figures.** Now is the time to double check your facts and figures—especially in your financial section.

4. **Check your layout.** The use of predefined styles can also make the process easier. However, layouts can wander off track during the entire process. To make your plan more visually appealing and professional looking, you should:

   a. Verify your margin settings. You should have a two-inch left-hand margin to have ample room to punch or bind. Adjust your margin settings before you make any other layout changes.

b. Go through each page and verify the Roman numerals assigned to each section and subsection.

c. Look for orphans and widows in your layout. An orphan is single word on the last line at the bottom of a page. A widow is a single word or short phrase at the top of a page. Most word processors can be set to avoid orphans and widows.

d. Check for consistency in titles, subtitles and footnotes. Most documents will be written in the business standard font, Times Roman. You may have chosen another complementary font for your titles. If you make your section titles Arial Bold and your subsection titles Arial Italics, then all of them should follow the same convention. If titles are to be in all caps, check to see that each follows this standard.

5. **Create a Table of Contents.** Your Table of Contents will list each major section. You may also like to list select subsections if your plan is longer than ten pages. Microsoft Word has a table of contents feature but you may find it easier to print out your full report and write your own. This is also a good time to verify your page numbering accuracy for inserts that were created separately.

6. **Inserting cross-reference information.** If you refer to a section/subsection or specific support document, you

may want to insert the final page number along with the originating reference. Since you've verified your page numbering system, you'll now know the correct page to direct the reader.

DO NOT SKIP THE FOLLOWING STEP

7. **Create a backup and hard copies of all word processing, spreadsheet, accounting and other documents.** Don't forget to include any research documents on your computer and even bookmarked Web sites. This backup should be stored (along with your work-in-progress backups) in a secure location. You've put a lot of work into this project so don't put that time and effort at risk. A hard-copy of your entire plan and all support documents is also be a wise idea.

    a. Floppy disks are the least secure method for backups. Burning a CD is a better choice. If you have a DVD burner, your data has even less chance of becoming inaccessible.

    b. When burning a CD or DVD, carefully review your CD/DVD creation software for the format that can be read by the most drives. Some formatting choices create disks that can only be opened on the same drive that created them. Don't assume that you'll be using the same computer when an emergency occurs and you need what's on the disk.

    c. Don't forget to open and look at your backup. Don't assume it was saved properly.

d. If possible, use another computer to look at your backup to verify that the documents can be accessed.

Making a Great Presentation

Your finished business plan is your salesperson. Just as you'd expect to dress appropriately during a sales presentation to a wealthy investor or a business banker, your plan needs the same visual image. Thanks to computers, inexpensive printers and readily available do-it-yourself presentation supplies, your plan can look clean, crisp and professional. Your first step is to decide how you are going to print it out.

Ready to Print

If you own a laser printer or top-quality inkjet printer, printing your entire document in the best or highest resolution offered is pretty straightforward. Often printer default settings are set at medium or better quality to conserve ink. This is okay for most tasks, but why worry about the cost of a little extra ink when you are printing something so important.

If you have graphs, charts or other support documents where color would improve the presentation, a color inkjet or color laser on the highest quality setting can be a plus.

If you don't have a printer with a quality output or need a color laser output, you can take your document on floppy disk or CD to your local self-service copy/printer store such as Kinko's®, a local computer lab or other office support/mailbox store. If your master document was created in anything other than the popular word processing programs, call first and ask what file formats can be used with their equipment.

Paper can be an issue at copy places as most won't let you print on anything but paper purchased from them. That shouldn't be an issue unless you want it printed on your existing letterhead.

Paper, Please

Once you have determined what equipment you'll print your plan on, you need to select a quality bond paper suitable for your chosen printer. Office supply stores have hundreds of options to choose from, so where do you start? Here is the minimum quality level you should use (this also applies when selecting paper at the copy store): white paper, 24 lb. (this is heavier and less opaque than ordinary printer/copier paper) with a 90 or above brightness rating (the higher the number, the truer the white). Select laser paper for laser output and inkjet paper for inkjet output.

If you want to kick it up a notch, check out the stationery paper section (usually near the paper reams) at your office supply store or ask the copy shop clerk to show you stationery or resumé paper. This paper is more costly than the high-end printer paper described above, but you may like the richness it adds to your presentation.

Select either 24 lb. white or ivory linen (no other colors, please). Linen refers to the visible grain used in more expensive letterhead. Mass-market stationery paper will also list whether it is laser- or inkjet-compatible. If in doubt, purchase the minimum quantity and take it home and test it. Linen and other quality papers have more absorbent fibers so your printer ink may bleed slightly, giving your document a slightly hazy appearance.

Holding It All Together

Before you head to the presentation folder aisle, you need to print out a mock-up of your plan on your chosen paper. This is so you can measure the thickness with any support documents you need to include. If your pile is an inch thick, a one-inch binder will be ample. If in doubt, select the next size up. Squeezing everything in just increases the chance that pages will be ripped. Business plans are one-use items (one person, one plan, no sharing), but why frustrate someone when you don't have to.

If you haven't put together a bound presentation in a while, you'll be amazed at the options. There are ring binders, folders with windows, leather binders, folders with pockets, folders that have plastic sheet protectors and more (no sheet protectors, please). The three-ring format is standardized so any three-hole punch will work. Look for a suitable binder or folder that looks expensive, but isn't. Colors such as black, dark brown, medium or dark blue and maroon are all acceptable. If it looks like your daughter would want to hand in her seventh-grade term paper in it, don't buy it!

If you have bulky support documents unsuitable for hole-punching, there are presentation folders that have pockets. Remember not to include anything that you'll need returned to you.

While You Are at the Office Supply Store

If you'll be mailing or shipping your plan, pick up an appropriate padded envelope or shipping box.

Assembling Your Plan

You have printed your plan on elegant linen paper, purchased a professional-looking dark gray folder and had full-color charts printed off. Now assemble everything together with your Table of Contents at the front (after your cover page). If your plan is over an inch thick, you might think about including section dividers with labeled tabs. These are available at your office supply store in a variety of formats including those that will go through your laser printer. Just make certain that you purchase the correct hole format and size for your ring binder and inserts.

Some binders come with a business card insert on the cover (front or inside front). Proudly place your card there.

12

Mini Strategic Plans

A trimmed down version of a traditional business plan can also be a powerful tool in decision-making and goal-setting. A mini-plan can be written for:

1. An introduction to your new restaurant venture. Suitable for preliminary discussions with bankers, potential partners and employee searches.

2. A specific marketing campaign. This can open a dialogue with an ad agency, marketing consultant and your restaurant managers.

3. A profit-enhancing plan. Use this to illustrate to employees how specific actions and changes can increase profits—which increase their salaries and bonuses.

4. Share your business goal-setting plan with employees at every level to collect ideas, build consensus, explain rewards and establish expectations.

5. Explore your personal goals and expectations. Should you delegate more to your employees and work less? Should you prepare to retire?

A mini-plan uses the same research and information-gathering techniques discussed earlier. If you are going to share the mini-plan with others, you'll need to have a structure and write with clarity and purpose just as with a full formal business plan. However, what you put in and how you express it, is much more flexible.

Half the purpose of any plan is to make you take the time to think about the reason for the mini-plan. It forces you to clear your mind and concentrate, which improves your decision-making abilities.

When you write your mini-plan, keep your audience in mind. Don't bore them with any unnecessary details. Whet their appetite, stimulate creativity and sell them!

Internal Business Plans

An internal business plan is written as an in-house decision-making tool and feasibility study. Will increasing your dining room size pay for the renovations required? How long would it earn back the cost of a $5,000 Italian espresso machine? Should you spend more money on radio spots or local cable TV spots?

To follow are some resources to help you create an internal plan that will excite your team, improve your decision-making and increase your chances for success.

- The Business Leaders Dream Tool—**www.leadership -tools.com/business-plan-template.html**

- Miller Consulting's Internal Business Plan Manual— **www.internalbusinessplans.co.uk/manual.htm**

- Sales & Marketing Strategies —**www.sms -direct.com/business-plan-development3.htm**

- BusinessCase.com—**www.businesscase.com /html/irr.html**

- Planware—**www.planware.org/strategy.htm**

- BusinessBalls.com—**www.businessballs.com /freebusinessplansandmarketingtemplates.htm**

Plan B entails reviewing where you can make changes.

13

Revising and Updating Your Business Plan

Plan B

You've just spent hours writing and rewriting your feasibility analysis (*Chapter 5 – What Does a Business Plan Contain?*) only to realize that the numbers just aren't there. The scenario may be that you won't have enough capital to keep afloat until you become profitable or the building you have selected won't seat enough people for the sales volume you need.

You are probably overwhelmed at this point. However, you still have opportunity to perfect your business model and increase your chance for long-term success. Restaurateurs who don't take planning seriously often stumble through this process with costly results.

What do you do? Create Plan B, of course. Plan B entails reviewing where you can make changes. Examine where your plan falls short. Do you need to rethink the renovation of a historic building? Do you need to delay your launch until you have an additional six months of working capital? Do you need to rein in your dreams and start out with a more manageable plan? Your research may reveal ways that you hadn't even considered. Perhaps a more casual style restaurant will be better suited for your community.

Money can be a big obstacle but not an insurmountable one. Millions of successful businesses start out on a shoestring and a promise of a future. There are two ways to conquer money issues: spend less or gather more.

- Look for ways to trim down your start-up needs. Perhaps leasing a building instead of constructing one. Purchasing used equipment instead of new.

- Look for more start-up capital. You can search for a partner, look for ways to live more frugally so you can add to your nest egg or seek out family or friends to invest.

Competitive factors can stall your plans. Could a different type of restaurant suit your desires and abilities and be a better choice for your neighborhood? The fourth pizza parlor in a three-mile range is probably not going to have ample customers for you to be profitable. Here is where you need to reexamine your restaurant concept. You can relocate to a more favorable location or you can alter your plan and open an Italian deli with a broader range of to-go meals.

A lack of customers can only be overcome by locating your restaurant in a more promising neighborhood or increasing your advertising efforts. Examine your demographic information. If there aren't enough of your ideal customers in the area, finding a better location may be your only solution. If there are plenty of potential patrons in your target market, you need to create an interest in your restaurant and bring more people in the door through advertising.

The key to Plan B is to find ways to overcome problem areas. Work with your accountant to run some what-if scenarios where different parts of your plan are altered so you can assess any beneficial changes. Search out advisors in your community who might have some creative solutions or give you a new perspective on your situation.

Keeping Your Plan Fresh and Viable

You've put a terrific amount of work into writing your business plan, so why not make it work for you again and again? Your business plan should be a living document that is reviewed and updated periodically. Read it over — have a good laugh if you must. You may discover that your vision was a bit naïve. Don't feel embarrassed — it's really a realization on just how much you've grown as a businessperson and restaurateur.

Does your restaurant resemble the description in your plan? Is it better than you imagined? Not as good? Are you successful in spite of not meeting the plan's goals? Do you see where not following the plan led you astray? Looking at what brought you to where you are and comparing it to your launch plan will help you make adjustments to bring you back on track or lead you into bigger and better things.

Your first business plan included your financial projections for the first three years of operation. Take your actual performance figures and see how reality stacks up. You'll also be able to do some updating based upon what you know now that you didn't know originally.

A good review schedule might be every six months during the first two or three years of operation. During the critical first three years, you may find it helpful to use the plan during quarter accounting reviews. By keeping your plan fresh, you'll be able to keep your original mission in mind. Other benefits to keeping your business plan up to date would be that you will always be prepared for growth, additional investment opportunities or to sell your business should the need arise suddenly.

At the end of three years, plans often need major overhauls to be relevant to current restaurant trends, the economy and competitive factors. Look at your plan as a guide to healthy growth. Revisit some of your assumptions. Are they still valid? Day-by-day business climates change and we often aren't even aware that they have. Thoroughly review how your restaurant was positioned over the past three years and set new goals for the next three to five years to help you stay profitable.

Some areas to revisit are:

1. Has the neighborhood demographics changed?

2. Have dining-out habits changed?

3. Have current food trends made your menu obsolete?

4. Did traffic flow patterns change your customer averages?

5. Would remodeling your restaurant bring in new customers?

6. Has your advertising brought in ample new customers?

7. Have you built a strong repeat business?

8. Are competitors outperforming you?

9. Have you outgrown your restaurant facility?

10. Should you add additional staff and personally work less?

Should You Rewrite Your Plan?

Businesspeople, who have embraced the power of a written plan typically revise and even totally rewrite their plan when its contents have become dated and irrelevant. This may be in a year or five years—only you can determine the value for yourself.

Rewriting your plan offers you the same benefits as when you created your first one:

1. **Clarity**—A clear view of your goals and the paths to reach them.

2. **Concentration**—Time set aside specifically for review, reflection and projection.

3. **Confidence**—Establishes what you do best and focuses on those skills and talents.

4. **Commitment**—Rededicating yourself, your resources and your team to a shared success.

Business Plan Writing Resources

Accounting

- Restaurant margin calculator — **www.heartlandpaymentsystems.com/Restaurant /Restaurant%20Margin%20Calculator.asp**

Advertising

- *The Food Service Professionals Guide to Restaurant Marketing & Advertising for Just a Few Dollars a Day* by Amy S. Jorgensen (Atlantic Publishing)

- The Barfly Group — **www.thebarflygroup.com**

- Restaurant Marketing — **www.restaurantmarketing.com**

- *Restaurant Marketing for Owners and Managers* (Wiley Restaurant Basics Series) by Patti J. Shock, John T.

Bowen, John M. Stefanelli

- Your Restaurant Marketing Genius at Work — download report at **www.RestaurantOwner.com /downloads/special_report.pdf**

- Other resources — **www.business.com/directory /food_and_beverage/restaurants_and_foodservice /marketing**

Books, Magazines and Software

- Bplans.com — **www.bplans.com**

- Atlantic Publishing — **www.librarybooks.biz** — food service books and software

- Restaurant Operators Guide to QuickBooks — **www.rrgconsulting.com**

- Megadox legal forms — **www.megadox.com /documents.php/97**

- Bulletproof Business Plans — **www.bulletproofbizplans.com**

- Bar business plan — **www.barbusinessplan.com**

- Ice cream parlor business plan —
  www.icecreambusinessplan.com

- Specialty coffee shop business plans —
  www.coffeebusinessplan.com

- Pizza restaurant business plans —
  www.coffeebusinessplan.com

Business Structure

- *Incorporating Your Business For Dummies* by The
  Company Corporation (For Dummies Publisher)

- TurboTax article "Should I Incorporate?" —
  www.turbotax.com/articles/ShouldIIncorporate.html

- AllBusiness Practical Guide to Incorporation —
  www.allbusiness.com/guides/Incorporation.asp

- Legal Spring consumer-oriented advice —
  www.legalspring.com

- Do-It-Yourself Incorporation

  - Business Filings Incorporated —
    www.bizfilings.com

- My Corporation — **www.mycorporation.com**

- Corporate Creations — **www.corpcreations.com**

Feasibility Study Resources
- Should I Start a New Business? — **www.mapnp.org /library/strt_org/prep.htm**

Financial Planning for Restaurants
- Virtual Restaurant — **www.virtualrestaurant.com** — spreadsheets, advice and planning tools

Food Service Industry Publications
- Restaurant Start-up and Growth Magazine — **www.restaurantowner.com/mag/index.cfm**

- Beverage & Good Restaurant Marketing Magazine — **www.restaurant-marketing.net**

- Nightclub & Bar Magazine — **www.nightclub.com**

Government Resources
- Small Business Association (SBA) — **www.sba.gov**

- Internal Revenue Service (IRS) — **www.irs.gov**

Industry Demographics and Research

- Biz Miner — **www.bizminer.com**

- National Restaurant Association — **www.restaurant.org/research**

- SBA — **www.sba.gov/starting_business /marketing/research.html**

Research Methods

- Web Surveyor — **www.websurveyor.com**

Restaurant Owner Support

- Restaurant Owner — **www.restaurantowner.com**

- Restaurant News — **www.restaurantnews.com**

- American Express — **http://home5.americanexpress.com/Merchant /resources/events/events_index.asp**

- Idea Cafe — **www.businessownersideacafe.com**

Small Business Development and Support

- Score — **www.score.org**

- Association for Enterprise Opportunity —
  www.microenterpriseworks.org — support for small (5
  or fewer employees) businesses with start-up costs of
  $35,000 or less

- Entrepreneur — **www.entrepreneur.com** — offers
  general business and restaurant specific guidance

- Bibliomaven — locate state and local business
  journals — **www.bibliomaven.com/businessjournals**

Training Classes, Seminars, Workshops and Web-Based Education

- NxLevel — **www.nxlevel.org** — free or low-cost business
  plan writing and entrepreneurial support training

- FastTrack — **www.fasttrac.org** — Spanish and English
  programs and information

Trade Associations

- All Candy Expo, National Confectioners Association —
  www.nca-cma.org

- America's Mart Atlanta — **www.americasmart.com**

- Barbeque Industry Association — **http://hpba.org**

- Dallas National Gift & Home Shows, George Little

Management — **www.glmshows.com**

- Fancy Food & Culinary Magazine — **www.talcott.com**

- Food Marketing Institute — **www.fmi.org**

- Gourmet News — **www.gourmetnews.com**

- Gourmet Retailer — **www.gourmetretailer.com**

- Institute of Store Planners — **www.ispo.org**

- In-Store Marketing Institute —
  www.instoremarketer.org

- International Daily Deli Bakery Association —
  www.iddba.org

- International Housewares Association —
  www.housewares.org

- National Association of Specialty Food Trade —
  www.specialtyfoodmarket.com

- National Association of Store Fixture Manufacturers —

www.nasfm.org.

- National Food Distributors Association— **www.specialtyfoods.org**

- National Restaurant Association Hotel-Motel Show— **www.restaurant.org**

- National Retail Federation—**www.nrf.com**

- National Specialty Gift Association— **www.nsgaonline.com**

- Natural Foods Merchandiser – **www.nfmtradezone.com**

- Natural Products Expo— **www.naturalproductexpo.com**

- New York International Gift Fair, George Little Management—**www.glmshows.com**

- Retailer News—**www.retailernews.com**

- Specialty Coffee Association—**www.scaa.org**

- Tea Association of American— **www.teausa.com**

- The Wine Institute —**www.wineinstitute.org**

- Trade Directory of Wholesalers—**www.thomasintl.com**

- Visual Merchandising Trade Association— **www.vmta.org**

Start-Up Expense Worksheet

Purchase Fixed Assets (building, land, equipment, vehicles)	$
Remodeling Costs (fixtures, signs, paint, cleaning)	$
Installation Costs (telephone, equipment, utility hookups)	$
Deposits (gas, electric, water, phone, building lease, equipment leases, workers' comp, etc.)	$
Fees, Licenses, Certifications, Bonds (business, resale, fire alarm, liquor, inspections)	$
Prepaids (property taxes, resale license, etc.)	$
Legal Fees (one-time start-up)	$
Accounting or Other Professional Fees (one-time start-up)	$
Goodwill or Franchise Payments	$
Pre-Opening Labor Expenses	$
Pre-Opening Training Expenses	$

Uniforms (rental or purchase)	$
Beginning Inventory of Ingredients and Resale Merchandise	$
Furnishings (dining room, bathroom, other public areas)	$
Dinnerware (glassware, silverware, dishware, serving utensils)	$
Supplies (letterhead, packaging, other consumable supplies)	$
Promotional Materials (opening house, giveaways, prizes)	$
Advertising (introductory advertising, media buys, direct mail, coupons)	$
Other Expenses (one-time, specifically related to start-up of restaurant)	$
	$
Total Start-Up Expenses	$
	$
Cash Available Now	$
Beginning Cash Balance or Cash Required (Cash Available Less Total Expenses)	$

15

Sample Business Plan

This chapter contains a complete business plan for a fictitious restaurant called The Oasis. Review this business plan carefully and compare it to your needs. This business plan is also included on the companion CD-ROM enclosed with this book. It is in Microsoft Word format and can be easily modified or used as an outline to suit your food service establishment.

"The Oasis"

April 2004

This Business Plan (copy number 1) contains proprietary and confidential information belonging exclusively to

"The Oasis"

Proprietor: Mr. Mark Readline
Phone: (217) 555-6598

(217) 555-4527

Contents

Executive Summary

This business proposal describes the plans for opening a restaurant to be called The Oasis, to be located at 1204 Lincoln Avenue in Charleston, Illinois. The objective of this proposal is to request a $90,000 working line of credit.

The Oasis will fill a unique niche in its market. Despite the presence in Charleston of 12,000 college students (the vast majority between the ages of 18 and 24), there currently exists no restaurant that combines convenience, affordability and healthy eating. The Oasis, a unique concept in quick-service restaurants, will offer all three, along with a hip ambiance designed to appeal to the college student market. The Oasis will offer create-your-own stir-fry dishes. Patrons will select the ingredients to be put into their stir-fry. Meals will be all you can eat—always an appealing concept for college students, yet given the nature of the product, an affordable goal for our restaurant. Our vision is "Fresh, healthy dining for the next generation."

The Oasis will enhance its reputation as the spot for college students on a date or wanting someplace fun but quick and affordable by creating a hip, funky indoor ambiance. A central rock waterfall will set a generally Asian theme. The back wall in the seating area will be surfaced completely in chalkboard, and colored chalk will be available so that patrons can "graffiti" the walls. No restaurant in a ten-mile radius offers anything like the fresh, new experience that The Oasis will offer to the college students at Eastern Illinois University (and, of course, to local residents).

The restaurant will be located at 1204 Lincoln Avenue in Charleston, Illinois, a property that has been leased from its owner, Martins Corporation. This location is on the "strip" directly across from the Eastern Illinois University campus. Lincoln Avenue is also Illinois Route 16, which connects Charleston with Mattoon, ten miles away, where it intersects with Interstate 57, which runs to Chicago.

The owner of The Oasis, Mr. Mark Readline, has managed a four-star restaurant and most recently was instrumental in a major revitalization of The Prairie House, a tavern-like restaurant in a historic building in the same region of east-central Illinois where Readline will now start his own restaurant, fulfilling a life-long ambition. Readline and assistant manager Karen Blair bring to this enterprise a wide variety of experience in the restaurant industry, two proven track records in all aspects of restaurant management, and in-depth knowledge of the market they are entering.

The Oasis will follow a two-pronged marketing

approach. Advertising focusing on college students will appear in relevant newspapers, and a variety of promotions will be targeted at the 18–24 year-old demographic. In addition, advertising will also appear in local daily newspapers, and promotions in conjunction with The Funky Bean, an established coffee shop, will target the older, permanent population of Charleston and Mattoon. "Fresh, Healthy, Hip" will be a slogan tying together all aspects of our promotional campaign.

The National Restaurant Association's 2004 forecast identifies health consciousness as the #2 trend in the industry for 2004. Extensive study of the competition in both Charleston and Mattoon suggests that neither of these communities currently boasts a restaurant that specializes in healthy dining. College students from Eastern Illinois University are known to travel as far as an hour away in order to find a restaurant they consider "nice" enough for a special date. The Oasis will fill a gaping hole in its market. We feel strongly that this is a safe business investment.

Statement of Purpose

This business plan is being prepared in order to secure a working line of credit in the amount of $90,000.

Description of the Business

With seating for 70, The Oasis will offer a unique, health-conscious, eclectic dining experience, featuring create-your-own, all-you-can-eat stir-fry meals. The unique dining experience at The Oasis begins with a walk through a salad bar-style buffet at which patrons select from a wide variety of fresh vegetables and other stir-fry ingredients, including a variety of sauces. Ingredients will include Asian-themed vegetables and sauces, as well as other flavor palettes (such as Italian-flavored sauces). Patrons then request beef, chicken, shrimp, egg or tofu to be stir-fried along with their selections from the buffet. The large grill will be visible from the patron side of the buffet so that patrons can watch and smell their meals cooking, but waitstaff will deliver the completed stir-fry (served with white or brown rice), drinks and desserts to the table. Although stir-fry will be the only main course offered, the ability to choose your own from the wide variety of ingredients will enable patrons to create a completely different meal every time they dine with us (and even on successive trips to the buffet during one meal).

The atmosphere at The Oasis will be hip, youth-oriented and casual, with bright primary colors accenting a primarily wood decor. Waitstaff will wear black pants or skirts and polo or T-shirts in one of a set of colors that complement the décor. One chalk-boarded wall will be available for patrons to cover with their own "graffiti" and drawings (and will feature inspirational sayings and jokes from the staff, rotated on a regular basis).

Restaurant hours will be 11 a.m. until 11 p.m. daily. The building that has been leased for the restaurant is a 4,060 square foot free-standing cement block building with seating for 70 customers (see floor plan). The building improvement contract and restaurant equipment orders have already been placed and delivery has been guaranteed for installation by April 1, 2004.

History

Since 1995, Mark Readline has managed The Prairie House, a mid-range, themed 100-seat restaurant adjacent to the restored 19th-century Carsey Inn in Carsey, Illinois. With a menu combining English pub food with American staples and a strong ambience based on the reconstruction of a 19th-century brick farm house and mill, The Prairie House was a well-kept secret when Readline took over as manager and initiated a marketing plan (in collaboration with the

Carsey Inn) to draw customers from new markets. First, in 1995–1997, Readline targeted the communities of Urbana and Champaign, Illinois, and later in 1999–2001, he expanded to another new market in Terre Haute, Indiana. With its new customer base keeping the restaurant operating at capacity every weekend, The Prairie House was able to introduce an expanded menu including some additional upscale items and to finance some long-needed renovations. Throughout his time as manager, Readline was studying the central Illinois market, in search of a niche for his own proprietorship.

Given his success with the central Illinois/western Indiana market, Mr. Readline was determined to find a need for a restaurant he could open as a single proprietor, and he found the opening he was looking for close to home: Charleston, Illinois, home to a 12,000-student university but no restaurants with a focus on the younger market. Readline had learned of this lack during his marketing campaign to draw Champaign/ Urbana customers to The Prairie House and had almost by accident found the Post House drawing a large customer base from the college students in Charleston. Having moved his family to Charleston to learn the community better, Mr. Readline realized the city offered few youth-focused dining opportunities and little in the way of variety of ambience or menu. After extensive study of the community and business environment, Mr. Readline developed a plan to open a restaurant that, like The Prairie House, would offer central Illinois diners a unique atmosphere and a menu unlike any of its local competitors: The Oasis, a specialty stir-fry restaurant with a casual but sophisticated décor and atmosphere.

Restaurant Name
The legal name of the restaurant is The Oasis.

Business Location
Mark Readline has leased the property at 1204 Lincoln Avenue in Charleston, Illinois, where The Oasis will be located.

Legal Form of Business
The legal form of the business is a Sole Proprietorship, as registered in the State of Illinois.

Founder
Mark Readline holds a B.S. degree in Hotel and Restaurant Management from Illinois State University. Since 1984, his career has taken him from his initial experience in management of a four-star restaurant in Chicago (Chef a l'Orange) to his phenomenal marketing transformation of The Prairie House. Since the age of 12, when he took over his mother's kitchen and proclaimed it "Chez Mark," Mr. Readline has dreamed of sole proprietorship of a restaurant. All of his

professional experience has been designed to help him learn how to make that vision a reality. With The Oasis, he is fulfilling a life-long dream.

Current Situation

With 20 years of experience in the restaurant industry and a well-developed business plan, Mr. Readline is well-positioned to start a new business that will flourish. As the marketing analysis in this business plan will amply demonstrate, The Oasis will fill a unique niche in a largely untapped market. With a unique concept and the ability to fill a genuinely unmet need in a healthy community, this restaurant has the potential to become a keystone business in its locale. Moreover, Mr. Readline's proven management and marketing skills, honed over years of improvements at The Prairie House, will be key to the success of this new venture.

The location on Lincoln Avenue in Charleston will benefit from retail traffic (popular businesses are located on either side of the restaurant's location; the only restaurants within three blocks are two fast-food restaurants). In addition, Lincoln Avenue becomes Illinois Route 16 outside of Charleston city limits, connecting Charleston with the larger city of Mattoon. Lincoln Avenue is therefore much traveled, so that the business's location will serve as a marketing tool in itself for residents of Mattoon who travel by it, as well as for parents and college students who travel this way to come in and out of Charleston going to and from campus.

The Future/Goals

Management's vision is to make The Oasis a keystone of dining options in the Charleston/Mattoon area within the first five years of operation. The primary clientele of the business will be college students, aged approximately 18–25, for whom eating healthily is a goal whether they are eating in or out—the National Restaurant Association's outlook report for 2004 identifies "heightened interest in health and nutrition" as the #2 industry trend for 2004. Our vision is "Fresh, healthy dining for the next generation."

Industry Overview

The restaurant industry has featured steady growth over more than a decade, reflecting trends toward convenience among U.S. consumers. According to Steven C. Anderson, President and CEO of the National Restaurant Association, "The restaurant industry remains the cornerstone of the nation's economy, career and employment opportunities, and local communities."

The following key facts are drawn from the National Restaurant Association's 2004 Industry Forecast:

- Restaurant-industry sales are projected to reach a record $440.1 billion in 2004, up 4.4 percent over 2003 sales, a real growth rate of 2.0 percent.

- 2004 will mark the thirteenth year of real sales growth for the restaurant industry.

- On a typical day in 2004, the industry is expected to post sales of more than $1.2 billion.

- Sales at quick-service restaurants (like The Oasis) are expected to grow 3.9 percent in 2004, to an estimated $123.9 billion.

- Although the Mountain region is expected to lead growth in 2004, growth in Illinois is expected to be close to the national average, estimated at 3.8 percent in 2004.

Creating a Competitive Edge with Setting

Over the past decade or so, one important trend has been the increased importance of design, décor and atmosphere in establishing a restaurant's position within a market. In recent years, restaurant owners have spent large amounts of capital in order to create a new resource for their business: a unique, memorable dining environment that both enhances the dining experience and creates a special niche for the restaurant. Setting, mode and ambiance are the newest area in which competitors seek to distinguish themselves.

The National Restaurant Association conducted a restaurant settings survey in 2000. According to the survey, restaurants with per-person dinner checks of less than $20 (like The Oasis), averaged $100,000 in capital investment in design and décor.

More upscale restaurants, not surprisingly, tend on average to make even larger capital investments in design and décor; according the National Restaurant Association's 2000 restaurant survey, restaurants with per-person dinner checks of $50 or more reported capital investment in design and décor averaging $400,000. The size of such investments, and the proportional increase in the size of investment as the cost of a meal increases, demonstrate how important atmosphere has become as part of the competitive marketplace. Investments in the dining environment are as critical to restaurant success as capital investments for kitchens (although capital investment for kitchen equipment was higher across the board than investments in design, according to the 2000 Restaurant Settings survey).

Given the significance of these investments, most restaurateurs turn to design professionals, both interior designers and architects. In particular, keeping the setting fresh and not "dated" seems important in the marketplace, with most respondents in the 2000 Restaurant Settings survey reporting that some level of remodeling had occurred in their dining areas during the four-year period between 1996 and 2000.

Setting Is More Than Walls and Furniture
According to a 2000 study commissioned by the National Restaurant Association, lighting, tableware, artwork and other materials all play a significant role in the dining experience and contribute to overall satisfaction. While food and service continue to be the most important elements contributing to the consumer's

overall satisfaction, the physical setting is also very important, and its importance varies with the kind of experience the consumer is seeking.

In general, the physical setting is of less importance at midscale or family-type restaurants where customers spend less time and are usually interested in just getting something to eat quickly. At the other end of the spectrum, upscale dining places—where diners are more likely to linger and make their meal more of an occasion—the setting is a very important part of the dining experience.

Outlook for Quick-Service Restaurants
Sales at quick-service restaurants are expected to exceed $123.9 billion in 2004, representing a 3.9 percent increase over the segment's 2003 sales level. In inflation-adjusted terms, sales at quick-service restaurants are projected to increase at a rate of 2 percent in 2004. The projected up-tick in real sales growth is the result of anticipated strength expected in the national economy.

Keeping Up with Customers
Consumers' insatiable desire for convenience continues to drive growth in the quick-service segment of the restaurant industry. As the number of employed persons in the United States continues to increase, the

amount of time left to prepare meals at home continues to fall. In fact, nearly 4 out of 10 adults (39 percent) reported in 2000 that they had decreased the number of meals they cooked at home during the preceding two years, according to the National Restaurant Association's 2000 Consumer Survey.

Quick-service restaurants are the natural segment of the restaurant industry that is best positioned to respond to consumers' increasing desire for convenience (and increasingly busy and pressured lifestyles). According to the 2000 Consumer Survey, nearly a third of adults (29 percent) indicated that purchasing takeout was "essential" to their lifestyle. For younger adults, the trend is overwhelming: nearly half of the respondents between 18 and 24 (47 percent) considered takeout food "essential" to their lifestyle.

The trend is clear: younger consumers feel even more time pressure than their already-busy older peers, so they value quick meals that they don't have to cook even more than their parents or other older demographics do. That means that quick-service is an obvious choice for a market including a large number of 18–24-year-olds.

Changing Consumer Needs

As with any market analysis, the ability to focus on consumers' changing preferences is critical in the quick-service market—particularly since customers tend to be repeat customers. In a 2000 National Restaurant Association survey of quick-service restaurant operators, more than two-thirds (76 percent) reported having introduced new food items in 2000, and 66 percent planned to add new food items in 2001.

As noted above, convenience is probably the most important feature that the quick-service segment of the restaurant industry offers consumers—a feature that quick-service provides in a way that more upscale establishments cannot. But the fast-food segment provides convenience too; often at lower prices. So quick-service restaurant operators cannot afford to ignore the importance of pricing and consumers' perception of value for the dollar.

One important response to the desire to combine value with convenience is an emphasis on promotions. According to the National Restaurant Association's 2000 Quickservice Operator survey, 82 percent of respondents offered weekly or monthly specials, making such specials the most commonly used promotion.

One trend that has yet to impact the quick-service industry fully is consumers' desire for healthy meals. Given the general emphasis in contemporary culture on health and weight control, fast-food chains have started trying to reflect low-carb and/or low-fat trends among consumers. Quick-service restaurants also need to follow this trend—a combination The Oasis is trying to forge.

Finding Good Help, Keeping Good Help

The labor pool for restaurants in general remains competitive. In most regions and settings, entry-level jobs are considered temporary work for the youth labor pool. That means that training and recruitment are critical.

After recruiting and training good help, though, restaurant operators often find that retention is nearly as big of a problem. Developing employee loyalty is as important to many restaurant owners as developing customer loyalty. Strong training and retraining programs, along with employee perks, are critical to maintaining a strong staff that offers high-quality service.

Competition

A survey of the competition clearly indicates that The Oasis will fill a unique niche in the Charleston/Mattoon dining market. In the mid-range restaurant category, all the competition in Charleston and Mattoon is focused on typical diner cuisine, with ambiance clearly targeting an older generation. No restaurant in Charleston or Mattoon offers a wide range of health-conscious meals featuring fresh and unusual vegetables, and there are almost no vegetarian dining options on the menus of any of the competition. Given that the National Restaurant Association's 2004 outlook report identifies "a continued focus on health and nutrition" as the #2 trend for 2004, and given that this trend is even more pronounced among the weight-conscious and health-conscious 18–24 year-old demographic, it's clear that a major opportunity is currently being missed by our competition.

Major Competitors

Our major competitors in Charleston are Kendall's, The Stallion Inn, and What's Fresh. Kendall's is Charleston's most upscale dining option. The menu is heavy on meat-based sandwiches and pastas, with a salad bar offering rather limited fresh vegetables. The average cost of a standard lunch selection is $5.95. The average cost of full dinners with salad is $11.95. Kendall's strength is its ambiance. Although the brass and stained glass clearly demonstrate that the last redecorating took place in the 1980s, Kendall's remains the "nicest" restaurant in Charleston. "Healthy" menu options are primarily limited to the salad bar; vegetarian options include the salad bar and a few vegetarian quiches. Kendall's hours are limited to lunch, served from 11 a.m. to 2 p.m., and dinner from 4 p.m. to 10 p.m., Monday through Saturday. Located on Lincoln Avenue, Kendall's will be the competitor located closest to The Oasis. Its exterior has a country appearance (blue-painted wood façade, striped awnings). The Oasis's more urbane exterior is designed to begin the process of differentiation from Kendall's at the curb.

The Stallion Inn is a local landmark in a historic building. The atmosphere is clearly typical tavern, with green plastic tablecloths and indoor/outdoor carpeting. The food and chef are known as the best in town. Ribs and steaks constitute their specialties, along with a host of grilled sandwiches and a few oddities like a frog legs dinner. The salad bar is even more limited than that at Kendall's, and vegetarian options are almost nonexistent: one portabella mushroom sandwich. The average cost of a standard lunch selection is $4.95, and a typical dinner selection is $9.95. The Stallion is open seven days a week, serving lunch and dinner from 11 a.m. to 10 p.m. For late-night weekend dining, The Stallion Inn will be The Oasis's primary competition. Our promotional efforts in cooperation with The Funky Bean are designed specifically to try to draw some of the late-evening crowd that might normally be headed to The Stallion Inn.

That's Fresh is the newest of the three major competitors in Charleston. Serving breakfast, lunch and dinner in a family-style setting, That's Fresh is best known in the market for baked goods, including its trademark strawberry bread. The average cost of a lunch selection is $7.95, and the average dinner selection is $10.95. That's Fresh will be The Oasis's primary competitor for the health-conscious customer. Much of the fare is standard diner food, but a few Mexican dishes, along with breakfast (served until 2 p.m.), offer vegetarian or at least more health-conscious options. That's Fresh tends to draw primarily local families, with students mainly attracted for breakfast. That's Fresh serves dinner only until 8 p.m. and is closed Sundays. The Oasis will primarily work to differentiate itself from That's Fresh through ambiance and newness.

Marketing Strategy

The Oasis's marketing strategy will be to position ourselves as the newest tradition for members of the Eastern Illinois University community as well as to market our excellent food and service in order to draw the local Charleston/Mattoon repeat customer.

Building and Signage

Given the highly visible position of our building, its exterior and sign will be critically important marketing tools. The exterior of our building (see supporting documents regarding building estimates) will set the tone of casual/sophisticated that will help establish our niche in the local market. Our new sign will be highly visible to both foot and auto traffic on Lincoln Avenue. Our landscaping will feature local prairie grass, providing a green front that will continue the tone of offbeat but relaxed sophistication; scattered floral plantings will echo the bright colors accenting the interior of the building.

Sales Strategy

We have established prices by taking into consideration the need to cover overhead while remaining competitive with Kendall's, The Stallion Inn, and What's Fresh. We have carefully reviewed those three competitors' menu offerings, and the price of our buffet has been set at the mid-range of local lunch/dinner costs. Our goal is to maintain a maximum 35 percent cost of goods sold and to maintain a net profit margin before taxes of over 15 percent.

Customer Service

Fast, gracious service will be critical to ensuring repeat business. In a small community with relatively limited formal dining options, word-of-mouth will be critical in establishing and maintaining a customer base, and establishing and maintaining an edge on the competition. Waitstaff will be thoroughly trained and new waitstaff lacking substantial food service experience will be eased into the business through a period of one month bussing tables and training, followed by one month hosting and training prior to waiting tables; this was a training strategy Mr. Readline found very successful at The Prairie House.

Advertising and Promotion

In order to attain our initial goal of serving over 200 meals per day, we will take a two-pronged approach to advertising and promotion, targeting our two major markets. In the month before our grand opening on August 15, 2004, we will target local media (the Mattoon and Charleston newspapers) and we will offer discount dining coupons through local radio stations and through a cooperative promotion with The Funky Bean coffee shop, located directly across the street from our new restaurant (the discount coupons will offer

$1 off a meal at The Oasis and $1 off an espresso drink or ice cream at The Funky Bean, during the first two months after our opening). These promotions, particularly since they occur before the opening of fall classes at Eastern Illinois University, will target local families and other permanent residents of Charleston and Mattoon.

The second major component of our initial advertising and promotion efforts will be directed toward the 12,000 students at Eastern Illinois University. We will advertise daily in the student paper during the first month of classes in 2004 (weekly thereafter) and we will offer a number of promotions targeting students from September through December 2004. These promotions will target Fridays and Saturdays, in order to establish The Oasis as a prime location for dating couples or for dinners before or after sporting events. Examples of these promotions include: a stir-fry sampler, allowing patrons to sample a variety of sauces and ingredients for free during set hours on Saturdays during our first two months of operation; free dinner for the first patron to come in after a football or basketball game and tell us the final score.

Our advertising budget of $1,000 per month following our first four months of operation will be spent on print and radio advertising in the Charleston/Mattoon/Eastern Illinois University media outlets.

Media Objectives and Strategy

Our primary objective is to establish our image as a hip restaurant offering fresh and nutritious food and a relaxed and fun atmosphere. We will maximize efficiency in the selection and scheduling of advertisements by:

- Selecting local publications with high local market penetration (the Times-Courier and Herald, as well as the Daily Eastern News).

- Collaborating with neighboring established business, The Funky Bean.

- Purchasing more ad space in the holiday and special events sections of local newspapers (the guide to the annual on-campus arts festival, the special insert on Charleston's yearly Octoberfest, etc.).

We will develop an advertising campaign built around our healthy menu offerings and location. We will support this plan with ads that reinforce the "Fresh, Healthy, Hip" slogan.

Promotional Campaign

"Fresh, Healthy, Hip"—this slogan will hold together our entire promotional campaign. By tracking the sales of promotional meals and by holding drawings for free lunches (in order to collect the names and addresses of patrons), we will be able to determine how well we are reaching each of the two major segments of our market.

E-Mail

The cheapest possible direct mail is e-mail. We will offer our patrons the opportunity to sign up to receive e-mail—coupon offers by e-mail on a monthly basis. They will also include one funny or thoughtful quote, and will be sent no more than once a month.

Publicity Strategy

Starting in July 2004 while renovations to our building are underway, The Oasis will focus on the following publicity strategies:

- Develop an on-going relationship with editors at the three local publications (the Courier, the Herald, and the Daily Eastern News).

- Develop a regular and consistent promotion programs targeting both local and transient (college student) populations.

- Produce a complete press kit to be used as the primary public relations tool for all target media editorial contact.

Grand Opening

The Oasis will issue a series of press releases prior to the grand opening on August 15, 2004.

Editorial Visits

Over the first two months we will invite the food editors of all local publications for a tour and complimentary review dinner.

Publicity Revenues

We anticipate at least 10 percent of our annual sales will be generated directly from our publicity. A full press kit will be sent to all local publications within the first two months of operation.

Community

The Oasis will sponsor a Charleston Little League Team in order to forge relationships with local families and residents. We will also participate in "The Taste of Charleston," a restaurant promotion held on Eastern Illinois University's campus each spring, to forge relationships with student groups on campus.

Operating Procedures

Location/Facility

The Oasis will be located at 1204 Lincoln Avenue in Charleston, Illinois, a 4,060 square foot building, to be leased from its owner, Martins Corporation. Mark Readline has negotiated a lease-to-own agreement with Martins Corporation, with a rent of $24,000 annually for the first five years. The size of the lot is 15,000 square feet, including a parking lot with 25 spaces. The facility is zoned commercial and is already equipped as a diner with full grill. The Oasis has budgeted and already selected bids for the remodeling of the facility at $16,750. The property is located on Lincoln Avenue in Charleston, Illinois; Lincoln Avenue is Illinois Route 16, which connects Charleston with Mattoon, Illinois, ten miles west, where Route 16 intersects with Interstate 57, which runs through Chicago to the north and Memphis to the south. Within a five-mile radius of this location are Eastern Illinois University, with 12,000 students and roughly 900 faculty and staff, and the Coles County Court House (Charleston is the county seat) with its associated legal offices and other commercial enterprises.

Licenses and Government Regulations

Local Regulations

The Oasis has obtained the following permits required for operations in the State of Illinois, City of Charleston:

Permits

We have received approval for renovation and submitted our remodeling plans to the City of Charleston for approval. Following is a list of permits and fees necessary to complete our remodeling plan.

Building Permit: Total estimate for renovations, $16,750. The fee is $125 with an application fee of $5 for a total of $130.

Electrical Permit: An electrical permit for these renovations will be required, at a cost of $200.

Plumbing Permit: A plumbing permit for these renovations will be required for $200.

Sign Permit: A sign permit will be required for $75 and an electrical permit of $27.50, for a total of $102.50.

TOTAL REMODELING PERMIT FEES ......$ 632.50

Zoning

C2, Commercial, Restaurant.

Health Department

Our kitchen design plans, operational plans, and menu for The Oasis have been reviewed by the Health Department and approved, contingent upon approval at a final inspection after completion of remodeling. The initial inspection cost $25, and the final inspection will also cost $25. When we pass our final inspection and pay the fee for it, we will be able to open.

Liquor License

We are applying for a Restaurant Beer and Wine Liquor license under the Charleston code that allows alcohol to be served with meals only in restaurants whose primary income is from food. The license costs $475 annually.

Fire Marshal

We have received preliminary approval of our renovation plans from the Coles County Fire Marshal's office. After completion of our renovations, we will pay $100 for our initial inspection and $75 in subsequent years for annual inspections.

TOTAL LICENSING FEES...............................$ 625

Utilities

Electricity: Amerens CIPS will require a deposit of $3,500 to activate electricity.

Natural Gas: To reestablish the meter and turn on service, we will pay a deposit of $400.

Telephone: Illinois Consolidated Telephone Company requires an initial deposit of $225 for both the fax and telephone line. A service fee of $48 is charged for the rerunning of phone jack locations for a total of $273.

Water/Sewer: The City of Charleston requires a deposit of $200 for water/sewer services.

Garbage/Waste Removal/Recycling: We will require a garbage container and route service. We have tentatively contracted with Prairie State; they will require a deposit of $200 for the first container delivery.

TOTAL UTILITIES DEPOSITS AND FEES $4,573

Capital Expenses/Improvement Budgets

The $90,000 long-term (5-year) loan will be used for the following (see copies of all estimates in the supporting documents section).

Remodeling estimates

Carpentry $2,000.00

Flooring $3,500.00

Painting Interior $1,500.00

Painting Exterior $2,500.00

Landscaping $1,000.00

Fixtures...$1,958.00

Plumbing...$1,500.00

Subtotal...$13,958.00

Contingency (20%) $2,792.00

Total Leasehold Improvements...............$16,750.00

Equipment

Ceiling fans $750.00

Mirrors $100.00

Lighting Fixtures $1,000.00

Stone water garden central art installation..$2,000.00

Office computer system $2,000.00

Office Fax Machine $350.00

Art Collectibles/Decor $2,500.00

Signage...$2,500.00

Restaurant Equipment $63,800.00

Total Equipment $75,000.00

Furniture

Office Furniture $930.00

Tables, Four Tops, total (24).....................$2,040.00

Tables, Two Tops, (19)................................$880.00

Booth Seating $1,000.00

Chairs (70) $3,400.00

Total Furniture..$8,250.00

Total Capital Expenditures

Building Permits $632.50.00

Licensing $625.00

Utility Deposits $4,573.00

Remodeling $16,750.00

Equipment...$75,000.00

Furniture $8,250.00

Total Capital Expenditures $105,830.50

Menu

The most important element differentiating The Oasis from the competition is the wide selection of healthy ingredients available for patrons to choose from, and the unusual flavor options of our stir-fry sauces. While seasonal specials will be offered in order to spark interest in returning customers, our staples will include a broad enough range to allow each dining experience to be special. Following is a price list and listing of standard offerings for lunch and dinner.

Prices

Vegetarian Lunch Stir-Fry
(includes egg and/or tofu) $5.50

Carnivore Lunch Stir-Fry (includes choice of beef, chicken or shrimp) $6.50

Vegetarian Dinner Stir-Fry $7.50

Carnivore Dinner Stir-Fry $8.50

All stir-fries include choice of white basmati rice, brown rice, or white-and-wild rice. Lunch and dinner prices both include unlimited trips to the stir-fry bar, and the rice bowl is bottomless.

Beverages

Iced tea, Evian, Coke, Diet Coke, coffee (all refillable)	$1.50
Wine (House Merlot, House Pinot Grigio)	$3.00
Beer	$2.00

Standard Choices on Stir-Fry Bar

Vegetables

Celery

Bok choi

Carrots

Cabbage (shredded)

Broccoli

Squash/zucchini

Baby peas

Miniature corn cobs

Tomato wedges

Green pepper

Red pepper

Jalapeño

Fennel

Cucumber

Snowpeas

Onion

Add-ins

Cellophane noodles

Peanuts

Sunflower seeds

Eggs

Tofu

Garlic (chopped)

Cilantro

Mint

Ginger (chopped)

Sauces

Plain soy (dark)

Low-salt soy

Ginger soy

Black bean

Hot curry

Mediterranean (balsamic/Italian)

Tomato spice (garlic)

Sweet chili and lemongrass

Coriander

Orange and spice

Hoisin

Meats

Beef

Chicken

Shrimp

Personnel/Service

The Oasis will be open 360 days out of the year from 11:00 a.m. to 11:00 p.m., and we will use three shifts of personnel led under the management of Mark Readline and Karen Blair.

Procedures/Controls

Cash Register/Till procedures

Given the simplicity of our menu, The Oasis will operate with a single cash register, operated by the host or hostess. Patrons will pay before proceeding to the buffet.

Inventory

Inventory will be conducted daily by the kitchen prep staff.

Personnel

As an experienced restaurant manager, Mark Readline understands the importance of strong management and active training of other personnel; therefore, he has carefully planned his management team to reproduce the success he experienced at The Prairie House. Day-to-day operational management will be conducted by Mark Readline and assistant manager Karen Blair, as hands-on managers covering all three shifts.

A supporting advisory management team makes up the Company's Board of Directors:

John Roed, Corporate Attorney

Corrine Maust, CPA

Ellen Barto, Restaurant Consultant

Mark Readline, Proprietor and Manager

Mr. Readline has had one dream his entire life: to own and operate his own restaurant. As a young boy, Mr. Readline took over his mother's kitchen, planning meals and only allowing the family into the room after he had welcomed them and "found" them a table. Through high school and college, Readline bussed and waited tables, cooked for three years at a demanding and busy New York City diner (Brownie's of Little Italy), studied the restaurant industry, and began a personal finance plan for amassing capital to open his own restaurant. In his first years after college, Mr. Readline served as an assistant manager at a four-star restaurant in Chicago (Chef a l'Orange), where he learned a great deal about niche marketing. When George Albinski, general manager of Chef a l'Orange, purchased The Prairie House in Carsey, Illinois, in 1995, he recruited Mr. Readline to serve as his manager. Jumping at the chance to prove his management skills, Readline relocated to rural Illinois and began to learn the local market. His marketing plans to expand into nearby markets with large suburban populations (first Urbana/Champaign and then Terre Haute, Indiana), boosted seat turnover dramatically, until The Prairie House was operating at maximum capacity every weekend. Profits at the Post House increased every year while Readline served as manager.

Meanwhile, Mark was learning the restaurant market in the surrounding central Illinois area. He heard repeated complaints from friends and neighbors about the paucity of dining options in the county seat, Charleston, Illinois, also home to a local public university, Eastern Illinois University, a 12,000-student, Division II sports team university. Friends who visited their sons and daughters who were students at the University complained that they couldn't find a healthy meal in town, and that during the dinner hour on a Sunday, the only open restaurant was packed. Readline began to wonder where the college students went on dates, so he asked his friend Bill Crane, owner of Charleston's thriving coffee shop, The Funky Bean, to allow him to conduct a marketing survey. The result was that he learned that college students were so dissatisfied with dining options that they sometimes drove as far as an hour away in order to find a "date worthy" meal. He also learned that a lack of healthy food was students' main complaint about Charleston eateries. Clearly, Mark had found a niche where his dream to run his own restaurant could become a successful reality.

Karen Blair, Assistant Manager

Karen Blair has worked in the restaurant business since 1976, when she opened "Mama's," a funky, student-oriented diner in Champaign, Illinois. Mama's offered an eclectic menu seemingly at odds with the 1920s diner décor: Chinese, Thai, Italian, and then-trendy "health foods," including whole-wheat rosemary and thyme bread that became legendary, baked each morning on the premises. Karen opened Mama's while she was a college student (an English literature major), because she had already become responsible for feeding a group of about forty students who were living in a commune-style setting. By the time she graduated, Mama's had become big business, and Karen had to decide whether to sell the diner to teach poetry or devote herself to the restaurant industry. The rewards of feeding happy people were too tempting, and Karen became a restaurateur for life (though every menu she's every constructed includes at least one poem). In 1980, she completed chef's training at the Chicago Culinary Institute. In 1985, she opened a second "Mama's" in Terre Haute, Indiana, where she relocated her family. In 1996, Karen decided to "retire" from the restaurant business. Her husband Joe Blair had taken a position as the chair of the economics department at Eastern Illinois University. Karen and Joe moved to Charleston, and within a year Karen had founded "Town and Country Catering." By 2000, Town and Country was the leading catering firm in Charleston, specializing in large parties and campus functions. In 2003, Karen sold Town and Country and "retired" again. But when her new friend Mark Readline, manager of her favorite local restaurant, told her of his plans to open a student-focused, health-conscious restaurant in Charleston, Karen needed little coaxing to come out of retirement in order to serve as Assistant Manager.

Responsibilities

Mark Readline and Karen Blair will share responsibility for management of day-to-day operations and for overseeing menu development, purchasing, portioning, pricing and inventory control, including approval of all financial obligations, as well as monitoring staff and, if necessary, terminating employment.

In addition to the management of day-to-day operations, Mark Readline will:

- Plan, develop and establish customer service policies and objectives.

- Plan and establish employee-related policies.

- Manage marketing and advertising, as well as plan promotions.

- Manage working capital and perform financial forecasting, including budgeting, cash flow analysis, pro-forma financial statements, and external financing requirements.

- Prepare financial analysis of operations for guidance of management, including the preparation of reports which outline the company's financial position in areas of income, expenses and earnings based on past, present and future operations.

In addition to the management of day-to-day operations, Karen Blair will:

- Hire and train waitstaff.

- Arrange for audits of company's accounts.

- Serve as liaison with artists and poets to display their work.

- Serve as liaison with board of directors.

Administrative Salaries

Mark Readline ....$ 43,000 per year

Karen Blair ....$ 40,000 per year

Financial Data

The financial data provided below is based on conservative estimates. They assume that renovations will be complete by the end of July and we will be able to proceed as planned with our grand opening on August 15.

Below, we provide month-to-month operating budgets for the next five years.

The following are The Oasis's Five Year projected revenue goals based upon an average ticket for lunch $6 and for dinner $8 in years one, two and three, with a $0.50 increase on both lunch and dinner in years four and five. The goal is to increase seat turnover from 1 in year one for both lunch and dinner to 1.25 in year two, and 1.5 in years three, four and five.

Year	Daily Seat Turnover Lunch, Dinner	Gross Sales	Net Income After Taxes
Year 1	1, 1	$ 1,361,250	$ 116,383
Year 2	1.25, 1.25	$ 1,523,475	$ 162,408
Year 3	1.5, 1.5	$ 1,745,460	$ 237,416
Year 4	1.5, 1.5	$ 1,797,750	$ 242,056
Year 5	1.5, 1.5	$ 1,850,040	$ 245,931

Cost of goods sold have been calculated as a percentage of sales and will be monitored on a daily basis in order to maintain a 25 percent cost of goods sold for food and a 3 percent cost of goods sold for beverage.

Operating expense assumptions have been estimated conservatively.

Inventory is turned on a 3-day cycle as inventory is used daily within all categories and because our high use of produce requires rapid turnaround. Accounts payable are projected to be 30 days.

Capital Requirements
Mark Readline has invested $250,000 into The Oasis, but an additional $90,000 is required. The additional $90,000 represents a working capital line of credit necessary for operating capital and as a contingency fund. This loan has been calculated as a five-year loan at a fixed interest rate of 9 percent.

The $90,000 long term (5-year) loan will be used in combination with the owner's investment of $250,000 for the following:

Total Capital Expenditures

Building Permits...$632.50

Licensing $625.00

Utility Deposits $4,573.00

Remodeling $16,750.00

Equipment..$75,000.00

Furniture $8,250.00

Total Capital Expenditures $105,830.50

Repayment

According to the following conservative financial projections, repayment of the requested $90,000 operating capital line of credit should be feasible over five years. Should The Oasis fail completely, liquidation of equipment and furniture should cover the $90,000 line of credit.

Conclusion

Based on the attached financial projections and supporting documentation, we believe that this venture represents a sound business loan.

We are requesting a working capital line of credit in the amount of $90,000.

The Oasis Year One by Month Balance Sheet

Assets	Aug-04	Sep-04	Oct-04	Nov-04
Current Assets				
Cash	$551,621	$557,394	$563,167	$568,940
Investments	$0	$0	$0	$0
Inventory	$1,734	$1,734	$1,734	$1,734
Other Current Assets	$8,525	$8,525	$8,525	$8,525
Total Current Asset	$561,880	$567,653	$573,426	$579,199
Fixed Assets				
Building/Leasehold Improvements	$16,750	$16,750	$16,750	$16,750
Restaurant Equipment	$155,000	$155,000	$155,000	$155,000
Furniture	$48,250	$48,250	$48,250	$48,250
Less Accumulated Depreciation	($2,619)	($5,238)	($7,857)	($10,476)
Total Fixed Assets	$217,381	$214,762	$212,143	$209,524
Total Assets	$779,261	$782,415	$785,569	$788,723
Liabilities				
Current Liabilities				
Short-Term Debt	$24,568	$24,568	$24,568	$24,568
Accounts Payable	$66,107	$66,107	$66,107	$66,107
Notes Payable/Mortgage	$0	$0	$0	$0
Other Payables	$5,000	$5,000	$5,000	$5,000
Accrued Liabilities	$0	$0	$0	$0
Total Current Liabilities	$95,675	$95,675	$95,675	$95,675
Long-Term Debt	$88,807	$87,605	$86,393	$85,173
Total Liabilities	$184,482	$183,280	$182,068	$180,848
Owner Equity				
Owner's Equity	$250,000	$250,000	$250,000	$250,000
Retained Earnings	$0	$3,131	$6,268	$9,412
Net Income/(Loss)	$3,131	$3,137	$3,144	$3,150
Total Owner's Equity	$253,131	$256,268	$259,412	$262,562
Total Liabilities & Equity	$779,261	$782,415	$785,569	$788,723

Dec-04	Jan-05	Feb-05	Mar-05	Apr-05	May-05	Jun-05	Jul-05
$574,713	$580,486	$586,259	$592,032	$597,805	$603,578	$609,351	$615,124
$0	$0	$0	$0	$0	$0	$0	$0
$1,734	$1,734	$1,734	$1,734	$1,734	$1,734	$1,734	$1,734
$8,525	$8,525	$8,525	$8,525	$8,525	$8,525	$8,525	$8,525
$584,972	$590,745	$596,518	$602,291	$608,064	$613,837	$619,610	$625,383
$16,750	$16,750	$16,750	$16,750	$16,750	$16,750	$16,750	$16,750
$155,000	$155,000	$155,000	$155,000	$155,000	$155,000	$155,000	$155,000
$48,250	$48,250	$48,250	$48,250	$48,250	$48,250	$48,250	$48,250
($13,095)	($15,714)	($18,333)	($20,952)	($23,571)	($26,190)	($28,809)	($31,428)
$206,905	$204,286	$201,667	$199,048	$196,429	$193,810	$191,191	$188,572
$791,877	$795,031	$798,185	$801,339	$804,493	$807,647	$810,801	$813,955
$24,568	$24,568	$24,568	$24,568	$24,568	$24,568	$24,568	$24,568
$66,107	$66,107	$66,107	$66,107	$66,107	$66,107	$66,107	$66,107
$0	$0	$0	$0	$0	$0	$0	$0
$5,000	$5,000	$5,000	$5,000	$5,000	$5,000	$5,000	$5,000
$0	$0	$0	$0	$0	$0	$0	$0
$95,675	$95,675	$95,675	$95,675	$95,675	$95,675	$95,675	$95,675
$83,944	$82,705	$81,457	$80,200	$78,933	$77,657	$76,371	$75,075
$179,619	$178,380	$177,132	$175,875	$174,608	$173,332	$172,046	$170,750
$250,000	$250,000	$250,000	$250,000	$250,000	$250,000	$250,000	$250,000
$12,562	$15,718	$18,881	$22,050	$25,227	$28,410	$31,600	$34,797
$3,156	$3,163	$3,169	$3,177	$3,183	$3,190	$3,197	$3,204
$265,718	$268,881	$272,050	$275,227	$278,410	$281,600	$284,797	$288,001
$791,877	$795,031	$798,185	$801,339	$804,493	$807,647	$810,801	$813,955

The Oasis Year Two by Month Balance Sheet

Assets	Aug-05	Sep-05	Oct-05	Nov-05
Current Assets				
Cash	$627,161	$632,814	$638,467	$644,120
Investments	$0	$0	$0	$0
Inventory	$1,734	$1,734	$1,734	$1,734
Other Current Assets	$8,525	$8,525	$8,525	$8,525
Total Current Asset	$637,506	$643,159	$648,812	$654,465
Fixed Assets				
Building/Leasehold Improvements	$16,750	$16,750	$16,750	$16,750
Restaurant Equipment	$155,000	$155,000	$155,000	$155,000
Furniture	$48,250	$48,250	$48,250	$48,250
Less Accumulated Depreciation	($34,047)	($36,666)	($39,285)	($41,904)
Total Fixed Assets	$185,953	$183,334	$180,715	$178,096
Total Assets	$823,459	$826,493	$829,527	$832,561
Liabilities				
Current Liabilities				
Short-Term Debt	$24,568	$24,568	$24,568	$24,568
Accounts Payable	$87,355	$87,355	$87,355	$87,355
Notes Payable/Mortgage	$0	$0	$0	$0
Other Payables	$5,000	$5,000	$5,000	$5,000
Accrued Liabilities	$0	$0	$0	$0
Total Current Liabilities	$116,923	$116,923	$116,923	$116,923
Long-Term Debt	$73,770	$72,455	$71,130	$69,796
Total Liabilities	$190,693	$189,378	$188,053	$186,719
Owner Equity				
Owner's Equity	$250,000	$250,000	$250,000	$250,000
Retained Earnings	$38,001	$41,125	$44,256	$47,395
Net Income/(Loss)	$3,124	$3,131	$3,139	$3,146
Total Owner's Equity	$291,125	$294,256	$297,395	$300,541
Total Liabilities & Equity	$823,459	$826,493	$829,527	$832,561

Dec-05	Jan-06	Feb-06	Mar-06	Apr-06	May-06	Jun-06	Jul-06
$649,773	$655,426	$661,079	$666,732	$672,385	$678,038	$683,691	$689,344
$0	$0	$0	$0	$0	$0	$0	$0
$1,734	$1,734	$1,734	$1,734	$1,734	$1,734	$1,734	$1,734
$8,525	$8,525	$8,525	$8,525	$8,525	$8,525	$8,525	$8,525
$660,118	$665,771	$671,424	$677,077	$682,730	$688,383	$694,036	$699,689
$16,750	$16,750	$16,750	$16,750	$16,750	$16,750	$16,750	$16,750
$155,000	$155,000	$155,000	$155,000	$155,000	$155,000	$155,000	$155,000
$48,250	$48,250	$48,250	$48,250	$48,250	$48,250	$48,250	$48,250
($44,523)	($47,142)	($49,761)	($52,380)	($54,999)	($57,618)	($60,237)	($62,856)
$175,477	$172,858	$170,239	$167,620	$165,001	$162,382	$159,763	$157,144
$835,595	$838,629	$841,663	$844,697	$847,731	$850,765	$853,799	$856,833
$24,568	$24,568	$24,568	$24,568	$24,568	$24,568	$24,568	$24,568
$87,355	$87,355	$87,355	$87,355	$87,355	$87,355	$87,355	$87,355
$0	$0	$0	$0	$0	$0	$0	$0
$5,000	$5,000	$5,000	$5,000	$5,000	$5,000	$5,000	$5,000
$0	$0	$0	$0	$0	$0	$0	$0
$116,923	$116,923	$116,923	$116,923	$116,923	$116,923	$116,923	$116,923
$68,451	$67,096	$65,731	$64,356	$62,970	$61,574	$60,168	$58,751
$185,374	$184,019	$182,654	$181,279	$179,893	$178,497	$177,091	$175,674
$250,000	$250,000	$250,000	$250,000	$250,000	$250,000	$250,000	$250,000
$50,541	$53,694	$56,854	$60,021	$63,196	$66,378	$69,568	$72,765
$3,153	$3,160	$3,167	$3,175	$3,182	$3,190	$3,197	$3,204
$303,694	$306,854	$310,021	$313,196	$316,378	$319,568	$322,765	$325,969
$835,595	$838,629	$841,663	$844,697	$847,731	$850,765	$853,799	$856,833

The Oasis Year Three by Month Balance Sheet

Assets	Aug-06	Sep-06	Oct-06	Nov-06
Current Assets				
Cash	$698,469	$713,155	$727,841	$742,527
Investments	$0	$0	$0	$0
Inventory	$2,185	$2,185	$2,185	$2,185
Other Current Assets	$8,525	$8,525	$8,525	$8,525
Total Current Asset	$709,179	$723,865	$738,551	$753,237
Fixed Assets				
Building/Leasehold Improvements	$16,750	$16,750	$16,750	$16,750
Restaurant Equipment	$155,000	$155,000	$155,000	$155,000
Furniture	$48,250	$48,250	$48,250	$48,250
Less Accumulated Depreciation	($65,475)	($68,094)	($70,713)	($73,332)
Total Fixed Assets	$154,525	$151,906	$149,287	$146,668
Total Assets	$863,704	$875,771	$887,838	$899,905
Liabilities				
Current Liabilities				
Short-Term Debt	$24,568	$24,568	$24,568	$24,568
Accounts Payable	$96,923	$96,923	$96,923	$96,923
Other Payables	$5,000	$5,000	$5,000	$5,000
Accrued Liabilities	$0	$0	$0	$0
Total Current Liabilities	$126,491	$126,491	$126,491	$126,491
Long-Term Debt	$57,323	$55,885	$54,435	$52,975
Total Liabilities	$183,814	$182,376	$180,926	$179,466
Owner Equity				
Owner's Equity	$250,000	$250,000	$250,000	$250,000
Retained Earnings	$75,969	$85,368	$94,767	$104,166
Net Income/(Loss)	$9,399	$9,399	$9,399	$9,399
Total Owner's Equity	$335,368	$344,767	$354,166	$363,565
Total Liabilities & Equity	$863,704	$875,771	$887,838	$899,905

Dec-06	Jan-07	Feb-07	Mar-07	Apr-07	May-07	Jun-07	Jul-07
$757,213	$771,899	$786,585	$801,271	$815,957	$830,643	$845,329	$860,015
$0	$0	$0	$0	$0	$0	$0	$0
$2,185	$2,185	$2,185	$2,185	$2,185	$2,185	$2,185	$2,185
$8,525	$8,525	$8,525	$8,525	$8,525	$8,525	$8,525	$8,525
$767,923	$782,609	$797,295	$811,981	$826,667	$841,353	$856,039	$870,725
$16,750	$16,750	$16,750	$16,750	$16,750	$16,750	$16,750	$16,750
$155,000	$155,000	$155,000	$155,000	$155,000	$155,000	$155,000	$155,000
$48,250	$48,250	$48,250	$48,250	$48,250	$48,250	$48,250	$48,250
($75,951)	($78,570)	($81,189)	($83,808)	($86,427)	($89,046)	($91,665)	($94,284)
$144,049	$141,430	$138,811	$136,192	$133,573	$130,954	$128,335	$125,716
$911,972	$924,039	$936,106	$948,173	$960,240	$972,307	$984,374	$996,441
$24,568	$24,568	$24,568	$24,568	$24,568	$24,568	$24,568	$24,568
$96,923	$96,923	$96,923	$96,923	$96,923	$96,923	$96,923	$96,923
$5,000	$5,000	$5,000	$5,000	$5,000	$5,000	$5,000	$5,000
$0	$0	$0	$0	$0	$0	$0	$0
$126,491	$126,491	$126,491	$126,491	$126,491	$126,491	$126,491	$126,491
$51,505	$50,023	$48,530	$47,025	$45,510	$43,983	$42,444	$40,894
$177,996	$176,514	$175,021	$173,516	$172,001	$170,474	$168,935	$167,385
$250,000	$250,000	$250,000	$250,000	$250,000	$250,000	$250,000	$250,000
$113,565	$122,964	$132,363	$141,762	$151,161	$160,560	$169,959	$197,358
$9,399	$9,399	$9,399	$9,399	$9,399	$9,399	$9,399	$4,114
$372,964	$382,363	$391,762	$401,161	$410,560	$419,959	$429,358	$433,471
$911,972	$924,039	$936,106	$948,173	$960,240	$972,307	$984,374	$996,441

The Oasis Year Four by Month Balance Sheet

Assets	Aug-07	Sep-07	Oct-07	Nov-07
Current Assets				
Cash	$831,830	$853,883	$875,936	$897,989
Investments	$0	$0	$0	$0
Inventory	$2,499	$2,499	$2,499	$2,499
Other Current Assets	$8,525	$8,525	$8,525	$8,525
Total Current Asset	$842,854	$864,907	$886,960	$909,013
Fixed Assets				
Building/Leasehold Improvements	$16,750	$16,750	$16,750	$16,750
Restaurant Equipment	$155,000	$155,000	$155,000	$155,000
Furniture	$48,250	$48,250	$48,250	$48,250
Less Accumulated Depreciation	($115,236)	($117,855)	($120,474)	($96,903)
Total Fixed Assets	$123,097	$120,478	$117,859	$115,240
Total Assets	$965,951	$985,385	$1,004,819	$1,024,253
Liabilities				
Current Liabilities				
Short-Term Debt	$24,568	$24,568	$24,568	$24,568
Accounts Payable	$105,555	$105,555	$105,555	$105,555
Other Payables	$5,000	$5,000	$5,000	$5,000
Accrued Liabilities	$0	$0	$0	$0
Total Current Liabilities	$135,123	$135,123	$135,123	$135,123
Long-Term Debt	$39,333	$37,760	$36,175	$34,578
Total Liabilities	$174,456	$172,883	$171,298	$169,701
Owner Equity				
Owner's Equity	$250,000	$250,000	$250,000	$250,000
Retained Earnings	$183,471	$196,909	$210,353	$223,805
Net Income/(Loss)	$13,499	$13,444	$13,452	$13,460
Total Owner's Equity	$446,909	$460,353	$473,805	$487,265
Total Liabilities & Equity	$965,951	$985,385	$1,004,819	$1,024,25

Dec-07	Jan-08	Feb-08	Mar-08	Apr-08	May-08	Jun-08	Jul-08
$920,042	$942,095	$964,148	$986,201	$1,008,254	$1,030,307	$1,052,360	$1,074,413
$0	$0	$0	$0	$0	$0	$0	$0
$2,499	$2,499	$2,499	$2,499	$2,499	$2,499	$2,499	$2,499
$8,525	$8,525	$8,525	$8,525	$8,525	$8,525	$8,525	$8,525
$931,066	$953,119	$975,172	$997,225	$1,019,278	$1,041,331	$1,063,384	$1,085,437
$16,750	$16,750	$16,750	$16,750	$16,750	$16,750	$16,750	$16,750
$155,000	$155,000	$155,000	$155,000	$155,000	$155,000	$155,000	$155,000
$48,250	$48,250	$48,250	$48,250	$48,250	$48,250	$48,250	$48,250
($99,522)	($102,141)	($104,760)	($107,379)	($109,998)	($112,617)	($123,093)	($125,712)
$112,621	$110,002	$107,383	$104,764	$102,145	$99,526	$96,907	$94,288
$1,043,687	$1,063,121	$1,082,555	$1,101,989	$1,121,423	$1,140,857	$1,160,291	$1,179,725
$24,568	$24,568	$24,568	$24,568	$24,568	$24,568	$24,568	$24,568
$105,555	$105,555	$105,555	$105,555	$105,555	$105,555	$105,555	$105,555
$5,000	$5,000	$5,000	$5,000	$5,000	$5,000	$5,000	$5,000
$0	$0	$0	$0	$0	$0	$0	$0
$135,123	$135,123	$135,123	$135,123	$135,123	$135,123	$135,123	$135,123
$32,969	$31,348	$29,715	$28,069	$26,411	$24,741	$23,059	$21,363
$168,092	$166,471	$164,838	$163,192	$161,534	$159,864	$158,182	$156,486
$250,000	$250,000	$250,000	$250,000	$250,000	$250,000	$250,000	$250,000
$237,265	$250,733	$264,208	$277,691	$291,181	$304,680	$318,187	$331,702
$13,468	$13,475	$13,483	$13,490	$13,499	$13,507	$13,515	$13,522
$500,733	$514,208	$527,69	$541,181	$554,68	$568,187	$581,702	$595,224
$1,043,687	$1,063,121	$1,082,555	$1,101,989	$1,121,423	$1,140,857	$1,160,291	$1,179,725

The Oasis Year Five by Month Balance Sheet

Assets	Aug-08	Sep-08	Oct-08	Nov-08
Current Assets				
Cash	$980,130	$1,000,011	$1,019,893	$1,039,775
Investments	$0	$0	$0	$0
Inventory	$2,499	$2,499	$2,499	$2,499
Other Current Assets	$8,525	$8,525	$8,525	$8,525
Total Current Asset	$991,154	$1,011,035	$1,030,917	$1,050,799
Fixed Assets				
Building/Leasehold Improvements	$16,750	$16,750	$16,750	$16,750
Restaurant Equipment	$155,000	$155,000	$155,000	$155,000
Furniture	$48,250	$48,250	$48,250	$48,250
Less Accumulated Depreciation	($128,331)	($130,950)	($133,569)	($136,188)
Total Fixed Assets	$91,669	$89,050	$86,431	$83,812
Total Assets	$1,082,823	$1,100,085	$1,117,348	$1,134,611
Liabilities				
Current Liabilities				
Short-Term Debt	$0	$0	$0	$0
Accounts Payable	$82,376	$82,375	$82,375	$82,375
Other Payables	$5,000	$5,000	$5,000	$5,000
Accrued Liabilities	$0	$0	$0	$0
Total Current Liabilities	$82,376	$82,375	$82,375	$82,375
Long-Term Debt	$19,655	$17,934	$16,201	$14,454
Total Liabilities	$107,031	$105,309	$103,576	$101,829
Owner Equity				
Owner's Equity	$250,000	$250,000	$250,000	$250,000
Retained Earnings	$345,224	$357,366	$369,516	$381,673
Net Income/(Loss)	$12,142	$12,150	$12,157	$12,166
Total Owner's Equity	$607,366	$619,516	$631,673	$643,839
Total Liabilities & Equity	$1,082,823	$1,100,085	$1,117,348	$1,134,611

Dec-08	Jan-09	Feb-09	Mar-09	Apr-09	May-09	Jun-09	Jul-09
$1,059,657	$1,079,539	$1,099,421	$1,119,303	$1,139,185	$1,159,067	$1,178,949	$1,198,830
$0	$0	$0	$0	$0	$0	$0	$0
$2,499	$2,499	$2,499	$2,499	$2,499	$2,499	$2,499	$2,499
$8,525	$8,525	$8,525	$8,525	$8,525	$8,525	$8,525	$8,525
$1,070,681	$1,090,563	$1,110,445	$1,130,327	$1,150,209	$1,170,091	$1,189,973	$1,209,854
$16,750	$16,750	$16,750	$16,750	$16,750	$16,750	$16,750	$16,750
$155,000	$155,000	$155,000	$155,000	$155,000	$155,000	$155,000	$155,000
$48,250	$48,250	$48,250	$48,250	$48,250	$48,250	$48,250	$48,250
($138,807)	($141,426)	($144,045)	($146,664)	($149,283)	($151,902)	($154,521)	($157,140)
$81,193	$78,574	$75,955	$73,336	$70,717	$68,098	$65,479	$62,860
$1,151,874	$1,169,137	$1,186,400	$1,203,663	$1,220,926	$1,238,189	$1,255,452	$1,272,714
$0	$0	$0	$0	$0	$0	$0	$0
$82,375	$82,375	$82,375	$82,375	$82,375	$82,375	$82,375	$82,374
$5,000	$5,000	$5,000	$5,000	$5,000	$5,000	$5,000	$5,000
$0	$0	$0	$0	$0	$0	$0	$0
$82,375	$82,375	$82,375	$82,375	$82,375	$82,375	$82,375	$82,374
$12,694	$10,921	$9,135	$7,335	$5,522	$3,695	$1,854	$0
$100,069	$98,296	$96,510	$94,710	$92,897	$91,070	$89,229	$87,374
$250,000	$250,000	$250,000	$250,000	$250,000	$250,000	$250,000	$250,000
$393,839	$406,014	$418,197	$430,388	$442,587	$454,796	$467,014	$479,240
$12,175	$12,183	$12,191	$12,199	$12,209	$12,218	$12,226	$12,234
$656,014	$668,197	$680,388	$692,587	$704,796	$717,014	$729,240	$741,474
$1,151,874	$1,169,137	$1,186,400	$1,203,663	$1,220,926	$1,238,189	$1,255,452	$1,272,714

The Oasis Break-Even Analysis

Year One by Month	Aug-04	Sep-04	Oct-04	Nov-04	Dec-04
Fixed Costs					
Operating Expenses					
Accounting/Payroll Processing	$500	$500	$500	$500	$500
Administrative Salaries	$6,916	$6,916	$6,916	$6,916	$6,916
Administrative Office Expense	$500	$500	$500	$500	$500
Advertising and Promotions	$4,936	$1,000	$1,000	$1,000	$1,000
Bank Fees	$100	$100	$100	$100	$100
Loan Interest Expense	$675	$666	$657	$648	$639
Loan Principal Payment	$1,193	$1,202	$1,211	$1,220	$1,229
Insurance	$2,500	$2,500	$2,500	$2,500	$2,500
Exterminator	$200	$200	$200	$200	$200
Lease Payment	$2,000	$2,000	$2,000	$2,000	$2,000
Legal Fees	$200	$200	$200	$200	$200
License and Permits	$200	$200	$200	$200	$200
Payroll Staff	$16,540	$16,540	$16,540	$16,540	$16,540
Real Estate Taxes	$0	$0	$0	$0	$0
Repairs and Maintenance	$1,000	$1,000	$1,000	$1,000	$1,000
Taxes Payroll/FICA	$1,794	$1,794	$1,794	$1,794	$1,794
Taxes Payroll/FUTA	$235	$235	$235	$235	$235
Taxes Payroll/SUTA	$469	$469	$469	$469	$469
Telephone	$800	$800	$800	$800	$800
Trash Removal	$1,500	$1,500	$1,500	$1,500	$1,500
Workers' Compensation	$1,525	$1,525	$1,525	$1,525	$1,525
Total Fixed Costs	$45,783	$41,847	$41,847	$41,847	$41,847

Jan-05	Feb-05	Mar-05	Apr-05	May-05	Jun-05	Jul-05	Year 1
$500	$500	$500	$500	$500	$500	$500	$6,000
$6,916	$6,916	$6,916	$6,916	$6,916	$6,916	$6,916	$82,992
$500	$500	$500	$500	$500	$500	$500	$6,000
$1,000	$1,000	$1,000	$1,000	$1,000	$1,000	$1,000	$15,936
$100	$100	$100	$100	$100	$100	$100	$1,200
$630	$620	$611	$601	$592	$582	$573	$7,494
$1,239	$1,248	$1,257	$1,267	$1,276	$1,286	$1,295	$14,925
$2,500	$2,500	$2,500	$2,500	$2,500	$2,500	$2,500	$30,500
$200	$200	$200	$200	$200	$200	$200	$2,400
$2,000	$2,000	$2,000	$2,000	$2,000	$2,000	$2,000	$24,000
$200	$200	$200	$200	$200	$200	$200	$2,400
$200	$200	$200	$200	$200	$200	$200	$2,400
$16,540	$16,540	$16,540	$16,540	$16,540	$16,540	$16,540	$198,482
$0	$0	$0	$0	$0	$0	$0	$0
$1,000	$1,000	$1,000	$1,000	$1,000	$1,000	$1,000	$12,000
$1,794	$1,794	$1,794	$1,794	$1,794	$1,794	$1,794	$21,533
$235	$235	$235	$235	$235	$235	$235	$2,815
$469	$469	$469	$469	$469	$469	$469	$5,629
$800	$800	$800	$800	$800	$800	$800	$9,600
$1,500	$1,500	$1,500	$1,500	$1,500	$1,500	$1,500	$18,500
$1,525	$1,525	$1,525	$1,525	$1,525	$1,525	$1,525	$18,296
$41,847	$41,847	$41,847	$41,847	$41,847	$41,847	$41,847	$506,102

The Oasis Break-Even Analysis (continued)

Variable Costs					
Food COGS	$13,110	$13,110	$13,110	$13,110	$13,110
Beverage COGS	$4,471	$4,471	$4,471	$4,471	$4,471
Merchandise COGS	$0	$0	$0	$0	$0
Credit Card Expense	$1,042	$1,042	$1,042	$1,042	$1,042
Royalty Fees	$0	$0	$0	$0	$0
Professional Fees/Other	$200	$200	$200	$200	$200
Paper Supplies	$1,500	$1,500	$1,500	$1,500	$1,500
Total Variable Costs	$20,323	$20,323	$20,323	$20,323	$20,323
Income From Operations	$71,880	$71,880	$71,880	$71,880	$71,880
Income From Operations Analysis					
Contribution Margin	71.73%	71.73%	71.73%	71.73%	71.73%
Break-Even Sales Volume	$63,831	$58,343	$58,343	$58,343	$58,343
Sales Volume Above Break-Even	$8,049	$13,537	$13,537	$13,537	$13,537

$13,110	$13,110	$13,110	$13,110	$13,110	$13,110	$13,110	$157,320
$4,471	$4,471	$4,471	$4,471	$4,471	$4,471	$4,471	$53,654
$0	$0	$0	$0	$0	$0	$0	$0
$1,042	$1,042	$1,042	$1,042	$1,042	$1,042	$1,042	$12,507
$0	$0	$0	$0	$0	$0	$0	$0
$200	$200	$200	$200	$200	$200	$200	$2,400
$1,500	$1,500	$1,500	$1,500	$1,500	$1,500	$1,500	$18,500
$20,323	$20,323	$20,323	$20,323	$20,323	$20,323	$20,323	$20,323
$71,880	$71,880	$71,880	$71,880	$71,880	$71,880	$71,880	$862,560
71.73%	71.73%	71.73%	71.73%	71.73%	71.73%	71.73%	71.73%
$58,343	$58,343	$58,343	$58,343	$58,343	$58,343	$58,343	$705,60
$13,537	$13,537	$13,537	$13,537	$13,537	$13,537	$13537	$16,954

The Oasis Year One by Month Income Projection

Sales	Aug-04	Sep-04	Oct-04	Nov-04	Dec-04	Jan-05
Food	$52,440	$52,440	$52,440	$52,440	$52,440	$52,440
Beverage	$19,440	$19,440	$19,440	$19,440	$19,440	$19,440
Merchandise	$0	$0	$0	$0	$0	$0
Total Sales	$71,880	$71,880	$71,880	$71,880	$71,880	$71,880
Cost of Sales						
Food	$13,110	$13,110	$13,110	$13,110	$13,110	$13,110
Beverage	$4,471	$4,471	$4,471	$4,471	$4,471	$4,471
Merchandise	$0	$0	$0	$0	$0	$0
Total Cost of Goods Sold	$17,581	$17,581	$17,581	$17,581	$17,581	$17,581
% of Total Sales	24.46%	24.46%	24.46%	24.46%	24.46%	24.46%
Gross Profit	$54,299	$54,299	$54,299	$54,299	$54,299	$54,299
% of Total Sales	75.54%	75.54%	75.54%	75.54%	75.54%	75.54%
Operating Expenses						
Operating Expenses (without Depreciation)	$47,332	$47,332	$47,332	$47,332	$47,332	$47,332
Depreciation	$2,619	$2,619	$2,619	$2,619	$2,619	$2,619
Total Operating Expenses	$49,951	$49,942	$49,933	$49,924	$49,915	$49,906
% of Total Sales	69.49%	69.48%	69.47%	69.45%	69.44%	69.43%
Total Expenses	$67,532	$67,523	$67,514	$67,505	$67,496	$67,487
% of Total Sales	93.95%	93.94%	93.93%	93.91%	93.90%	93.89%
Income From Operations	$4,348	$4,357	$4,366	$4,375	$4,384	$4,393
% of Total Sales	6.05%	6.06%	6.07%	6.09%	6.10%	6.11%
Taxes on Income	$1,217	$1,220	$1,222	$1,225	$1,228	$1,230
% of Total Sales	1.69%	1.70%	1.70%	1.70%	1.71%	1.72%
Net Income After Taxes	$3,131	$3,137	$3,144	$3,150	$3,156	$3,163
% of Total Sales	4.36%	4.36%	4.37%	4.38%	4.39%	4.40%

Feb-05	Mar-05	Apr-05	May-05	Jun-05	Jul-05	Year 1	% of Total Sales
$52,440	$52,440	$52,440	$52,440	$52,440	$52,440	$629,280	72.95%
$19,440	$19,440	$19,440	$19,440	$19,440	$19,440	$233,280	27.05%
$0	$0	$0	$0	$0	$0	$0	0.00%
$71,880	$71,880	$71,880	$71,880	$71,880	$71,880	$862,560	100%
$13,110	$13,110	$13,110	$13,110	$13,110	$13,110	$157,320	18.24%
$4,471	$4,471	$4,471	$4,471	$4,471	$4,471	$53,654	6.22%
$0	$0	$0	$0	$0	$0	$0	0.00%
$17,581	$17,581	$17,581	$17,581	$17,581	$17,581	$210,974	0.00%
24.46%	24.46%	24.46%	24.46%	24.46%	24.46%	24.46%	
$54,299	$54,299	$54,299	$54,299	$54,299	$54,299	$651,586	75.54%
75.54%	75.54%	75.54%	75.54%	75.54%	75.54%	75.54%	
$47,332	$47,332	$47,332	$47,332	$47,332	$47,332	$567,380	65.78%
$2,619	$2,619	$2,619	$2,619	$2,619	$2,619	$31,428	3.64%
$49,896	$49,887	$49,878	$49,868	$49,859	$49,849	$598,808	69.42%
69.42%	69.40%	69.39%	69.38%	69.36%	69.35%	69.42%	
$67,478	$67,468	$67,459	$67,449	$67,440	$67,430	$809,783	93.88%
93.88%	93.86%	93.85%	93.84%	93.82%	93.81%	93.88%	
$4,402	$4,412	$4,421	$4,431	$4,440	$4,450	$52,777	6.12%
6.12%	6.14%	6.15%	6.16%	6.18%	6.19%	6.12%	
$1,233	$1,235	$1,238	$1,241	$1,243	$1,246	$14,778	1.71%
1.72%	1.72%	1.73%	1.73%	1.73%	1.73%	1.71%	
$3,169	$3,177	$3,183	$3,190	$3,197	$3,204	$37,999	4.41%
4.41%	4.42%	4.43%	4.44%	4.45%	4.46%	4.41%	

The Oasis Year Two by Month Income Projection

Sales	Aug-05	Sep-05	Oct-05	Nov-05	Dec-05	Jan-06
Food	$65,550	$65,550	$65,550	$65,550	$65,550	$65,550
Beverage	$9,000	$9,000	$9,000	$9,000	$9,000	$9,000
Merchandise	$0	$0	$0	$0	$0	$0
Total Sales	$74,550	$74,550	$74,550	$74,550	$74,550	$74,550
Cost of Sales						
Food	$16,388	$16,388	$16,388	$16,388	$16,388	$16,388
Beverage	$2,070	$2,070	$2,070	$2,070	$2,070	$2,070
Merchandise	$0	$0	$0	$0	$0	$0
Total Cost of Goods Sold	$18,458	$18,458	$18,458	$18,458	$18,458	$18,458
% of Total Sales	24.76%	24.76%	24.76%	24.76%	24.76%	24.76%
Gross Profit	$56,093	$56,09	$56,09	$56,09	$56,09	$56,09
% of Total Sales	75.24%	75.24%	75.24%	75.24%	75.24%	75.24%
Operating Expenses						
Operating Expenses (without Depreciation)	$49,135	$49,125	$49,115	$49,105	$49,095	$49,085
Depreciation	$2,619	$2,619	$2,619	$2,619	$2,619	$2,619
Total Operating Expenses	$51,754	$51,744	$51,734	$51,724	$51,714	$51,704
% of Total Sales	69.42%	69.41%	69.39%	69.38%	69.37%	69.35%
Total Expenses	$70,211	$70,201	$70,191	$70,181	$70,171	$70,161
% of Total Sales	94.18%	94.17%	94.15%	94.14%	94.13%	94.11%
Income From Operations	$4,339	$4,349	$4,359	$4,369	$4,379	$4,389
% of Total Sales	5.82%	5.83%	5.85%	5.86%	5.87%	5.89%
Taxes on Income	$1,215	$1,218	$1,222	$1,220	$1,223	$1,226
% of Total Sales	1.63%	1.63%	1.64%	1.64%	1.64%	1.65%
Net Income After Taxes	$3,124	$3,131	$3,139	$3,146	$3,153	$3,160
% of Total Sales	4.19%	4.20%	4.21%	4.22%	4.23%	4.24%

Feb-06	Mar-06	Apr-06	May-06	Jun-06	Jul-06	Year 2	% of Total Sales
$65,550	$65,550	$65,550	$65,550	$65,550	$65,55	$786,600	87.93%
$9,000	$9,000	$9,000	$9,000	$9,000	$9,000	$180,000	12.07%
$0	$0	$0	$0	$0	$0	$0	0.00%
$74,550	$74,550	$74,550	$74,550	$74,550	$74,550	$894,600	100%
$16,388	$16,388	$16,388	$16,388	$16,388	$16,388	$196,650	21.98%
$2,070	$2,070	$2,070	$2,070	$2,070	$2,070	$24,840	2.78%
$0	$0	$0	$0	$0	$0	$0	0.00%
$18,458	$18,458	$18,458	$18,458	$18,458	$18,458	$221,490	24.76%
24.76%	24.76%	24.76%	24.76%	24.76%	24.76%	24.76%	
$56,09	$56,09	$56,09	$56,09	$56,09	$56,09	$673,910	75.24%
75.24%	75.24%	75.24%	75.24%	75.24%	75.24%	75.24%	
$49,075	$49,064	$49,054	$49,044	$49,033	$49,023	$588,952	65.83%
$2,619	$2,619	$2,619	$2,619	$2,619	$2,619	$31,428	3.51%
$51,694	$51,683	$51,673	$51,663	$51,652	$51,642	$620,380	69.35%
69.34%	69.33%	69.31%	69.30%	69.29%	69.27%	69.35%	
$70,151	$70,141	$70,131	$70,120	$70,110	$70,099	$841,870	94.11%
94.10%	94.09%	94.07%	94.06%	94.04%	94.03%	94.11%	
$4,399	$4,409	$4,419	$4,430	$4,440	$4,451	$52,730	5.89%
5.90%	5.91%	5.93%	5.94%	5.96%	5.97%	5.89%	
$1,229	$1,232	$1,234	$1,237	$1,240	$1,247	$14,764	1.65%
1.65%	1.66%	1.66%	1.66%	1.67%	1.67%	1.65%	
$3,167	$3,175	$3,182	$3,190	$3,197	$3,204	$37,966	4.24%
4.25%	4.26%	4.27%	4.28%	4.29%	4.30%	4.24%	

The Oasis Year Three by Month Income Projection

Sales	Aug-06	Sep-06	Oct-06	Nov-06	Dec-06	Jan-07
Food	$78,660	$78,660	$78,660	$78,660	$78,660	$78,660
Beverage	$10,800	$10,800	$10,800	$10,800	$10,800	$10,800
Merchandise	$0	$0	$0	$0	$0	$0
Total Sales	$89,460	$89,460	$89,460	$89,460	$89,460	$89,460
Cost of Sales						
Food	$19,665	$19,665	$19,665	$19,665	$19,665	$19,665
Beverage	$2,484	$2,484	$2,484	$2,484	$2,484	$2,484
Merchandise	$0	$0	$0	$0	$0	$0
Total Cost of Goods Sold	$22,149	$22,149	$22,149	$22,149	$22,149	$22,149
% of Total Sales	24.76%	24.76%	24.76%	24.76%	24.76%	24.76%
Gross Profit	$67,311	$67,311	$67,311	$67,311	$67,311	$67,311
% of Total Sales	75.24%	75.24%	75.24%	75.24%	75.24%	75.24%
Operating Expenses						
Operating Expenses (without Depreciation)	$51,198	$51,187	$51,176	$51,165	$51,154	$51,143
Depreciation	$2,619	$2,619	$2,619	$2,619	$2,619	$2,619
Total Operating Expenses	$53,817	$53,806	$53,795	$53,784	$53,773	$53,762
% of Total Sales	60.16%	60.15%	60.13%	60.12%	60.11%	60.10%
Total Expenses	$75,966	$75,955	$75,944	$75,933	$75,922	$75,911
% of Total Sales	84.92%	84.90%	84.89%	84.88%	84.87%	84.86%
Income From Operations	$13,494	$13,505	$13,516	$13,527	$13,538	$13,549
% of Total Sales	15.08%	15.10%	15.11%	15.12%	15.13%	15.14%
Taxes on Income	$4,858	$4,862	$4,866	$4,870	$4,874	$4,877
% of Total Sales	5.43%	5.43%	5.44%	5.44%	5.45%	5.45%
Net Income After Taxes	$8,636	$8,643	$8,650	$8,657	$8,664	$8,672
% of Total Sales	9.65%	9.66%	9.67%	9.68%	9.68%	9.69%

Feb-07	Mar-07	Apr-07	May-07	Jun-07	Jul-07	Year 3	% of Total Sales
$78,660	$78,660	$78,660	$78,660	$78,660	$78,660	$943,920	87.93%
$10,800	$10,800	$10,800	$10,800	$10,800	$10,800	$129,600	12.07%
$0	$0	$0	$0	$0	$0	$0	0.00%
$89,460	$89,460	$89,460	$89,460	$89,460	$89,460	$1,073,520	100%
$19,665	$19,665	$19,665	$19,665	$19,665	$19,665	$235,980	21.98%
$2,484	$2,484	$2,484	$2,484	$2,484	$2,484	$29,808	2.78%
$0	$0	$0	$0	$0	$0	$0	0.00%
$22,149	$22,149	$22,149	$22,149	$22,149	$22,149	$265,788	24.76%
24.76%	24.76%	24.76%	24.76%	24.76%	24.76%	24.76%	
$67,311	$67,311	$67,311	$67,311	$67,311	$67,311	$807,732	75.24%
75.24%	75.24%	75.24%	75.24%	75.24%	75.24%	75.24%	
$51,132	$51,121	$51,110	$51,098	$51,087	$51,075	$613,648	57.16%
$2,619	$2,619	$2,619	$2,619	$2,619	$2,619	$31,428	2.93%
$53,751	$53,740	$53,729	$53,717	$53,706	$53,694	$645,076	60.09%
60.08%	60.07%	60.06%	60.05%	60.03%	60.02%	60.09%	
$75,900	$75,889	$75,878	$75,866	$75,855	$75,843	$910,864	84.85%
84.84%	84.83%	84.82%	84.80%	84.79%	84.78%	84.85%	
$13,560	$13,571	$13,582	$13,594	$13,605	$13,605	$162,656	15.15%
15.16%	15.17%	15.18%	15.20%	15.21%	15.22%	15.15%	
$4,881	$4,886	$4,890	$4,894	$4,898	$4,900	$58,556	5.45%
5.46%	5.46%	5.47%	5.47%	5.48%	5.48%	5.45%	
$8,679	$8,685	$8,692	$8,700	$8,707	$8,717	$104,100	9.70%
9.70%	9.71%	9.72%	9.73%	9.73%	9.74%	9.70%	

The Oasis Year Four by Month Income Projection

Sales	Aug-07	Sep-07	Oct-07	Nov-07	Dec-07	Jan-08
Food	$90,795	$90,795	$90,795	$90,795	$90,795	$90,795
Beverage	$11,475	$11,475	$11,475	$11,475	$11,475	$11,475
Merchandise	$0	$0	$0	$0	$0	$0
Total Sales	$102,270	$102,270	$102,270	$102,270	$102,270	$102,270
Cost of Sales						
Food	$22,699	$22,699	$22,699	$22,699	$22,699	$22,699
Beverage	$2,639	$2,639	$2,639	$2,639	$2,639	$2,639
Merchandise	$0	$0	$0	$0	$0	$0
Total Cost of Goods Sold	$25,338	$25,338	$25,338	$25,338	$25,338	$25,338
% of Total Sales	24.78%	24.78%	24.78%	24.78%	24.78%	24.78%
Gross Profit	$76,932	$76,932	$76,932	$76,932	$76,932	$76,932
% of Total Sales	75.22%	75.22%	75.22%	75.22%	75.22%	75.22%
Operating Expenses						
Operating Expenses (without Depreciation)	$53,317	$53,306	$53,294	$53,282	$53,270	$53,258
Depreciation	$2,619	$2,619	$2,619	$2,619	$2,619	$2,619
Total Operating Expenses	$55,936	$55,925	$55,913	$55,901	$55,889	$55,877
% of Total Sales	54.69%	54.68%	54.67%	54.66%	54.65%	54.64%
Total Expenses	$81,274	$81,263	$81,251	$81,239	$81,227	$81,215
% of Total Sales	79.47%	79.46%	79.45%	79.44%	79.42%	79.41%
Income From Operations	$20,996	$21,007	$21,019	$21,031	$21,043	$21,055
% of Total Sales	20.53%	20.54%	20.55%	20.56%	20.58%	20.59%
Taxes on Income	$7,558	$7,563	$7,567	$7,571	$7,575	$7,580
% of Total Sales	7.39%	7.40%	7.40%	7.40%	7.41%	7.41%
Net Income After Taxes	$13,438	$13,444	$13,452	$13,460	$13,468	$13,475
% of Total Sales	13.14%	13.15%	13.15%	13.16%	13.17%	13.18%

Feb-08	Mar-08	Apr-08	May-08	Jun-08	Jul-08	Year 4	% of Total Sales
$90,795	$90,795	$90,795	$90,795	$90,795	$90,795	$1,089,540	88.78%
$11,475	$11,475	$11,475	$11,475	$11,475	$11,475	$137,700	11.22%
$0	$0	$0	$0	$0	$0	$0	0.00%
$102,270	$102,270	$102,270	$102,270	$102,270	$102,270	$1,227,240	100%
$22,699	$22,699	$22,699	$22,699	$22,699	$22,699	$272,385	21.98%
$2,639	$2,639	$2,639	$2,639	$2,639	$2,639	$31,671	2.58%
$0	$0	$0	$0	$0	$0	$0	0.00%
$25,338	$25,338	$25,338	$25,338	$25,338	$25,338	$304,056	24.78%
24.78%	24.78%	24.78%	24.78%	24.78%	24.78%	24.78%	
$76,932	$76,932	$76,932	$76,932	$76,932	$76,932	$923,184	75.22%
75.22%	75.22%	75.22%	75.22%	75.22%	75.22%	75.22%	
$53,246	$53,234	$53,221	$53,209	$53,196	$53,184	$639,017	52.07%
$2,619	$2,619	$2,619	$2,619	$2,619	$2,619	$31,428	2.56%
$55,865	$55,853	$55,840	$55,828	$55,815	$55,803	$670,445	54.63%
54.63%	54.61%	54.60%	54.59%	54.58%	54.56%	54.63%	
$81,203	$81,191	$81,178	$81,166	$81,153	$81,141	$974,501	79.41%
79.40%	79.39%	79.41%	79.38%	79.36%	79.35%	79.41%	
$21,067	$21,079	$21,092	$21,104	$21,117	$21,129	$252,739	20.59%
20.60%	20.61%	20.62%	20.64%	20.65%	20.66%	20.59%	
$7,584	$7,589	$7,593	$7,597	$7,602	$7,607	$90,986	7.41%
7.42%	7.42%	7.42%	7.43%	7.43%	7.44%	7.41%	
$13,483	$13,490	$13,499	$13,507	$13,515	$13,522	$161,753	13.18%
13.18%	13.19%	13.20%	13.21%	13.22%	13.22%	13.18%	

The Oasis Year Five by Month Income Projection

Sales	Aug-08	Sep-08	Oct-08	Nov-08	Dec-08	Jan-09
Food	$90,795	$90,795	$90,795	$90,795	$90,795	$90,795
Beverage	$11,475	$11,475	$11,475	$11,475	$11,475	$11,475
Merchandise	$0	$0	$0	$0	$0	$0
Total Sales	$102,270	$102,270	$102,270	$102,270	$102,270	$102,270
Cost of Sales						
Food	$22,699	$22,699	$22,699	$22,699	$22,699	$22,699
Beverage	$2,639	$2,639	$2,639	$2,639	$2,639	$2,639
Merchandise	$0	$0	$0	$0	$0	$0
Total Cost of Goods Sold	$25,338	$25,338	$25,338	$25,338	$25,338	$25,338
% of Total Sales	24.78%	24.78%	24.78%	24.78%	24.78%	24.78%
Gross Profit	$76,932	$76,932	$76,932	$76,932	$76,932	$76,932
% of Total Sales	75.22%	75.22%	75.22%	75.22%	75.22%	75.22%
Operating Expenses						
Operating Expenses (without Depreciation)	$55,342	$55,329	$55,317	$55,304	$55,290	$55,277
Depreciation	$2,619	$2,619	$2,619	$2,619	$2,619	$2,619
Total Operating Expenses	$57,961	$57,619	$57,936	$57,923	$57,909	$57,896
% of Total Sales	56.67%	56.66%	56.65%	56.64%	56.62%	56.61%
Total Expenses	$83,299	$83,286	$83,274	$83,261	$83,247	$83,234
% of Total Sales	81.45%	81.44%	81.43%	81.41%	81.40%	81.39%
Income From Operations	$18,971	$18,984	$18,996	$19,009	$19,023	$19,036
% of Total Sales	18.55%	18.56%	18.57%	18.59%	18.60%	18.61%
Taxes on Income	$6,829	$6,834	$6,839	$6,843	$6,848	$6,853
% of Total Sales	6.68%	6.68%	6.69%	6.69%	6.70%	6.70%
Net Income After Taxes	$12,142	$12,150	$12,157	$12,166	$12,175	$12,183
% of Total Sales	11.87%	11.88%	11.89%	11.90%	11.90%	11.91%

Feb-09	Mar-09	Apr-09	May-09	Jun-09	Jul-09	Year 5	% of Total Sales
$90,795	$90,795	$90,795	$90,795	$90,795	$90,795	$1,089,540	88.78%
$11,475	$11,475	$11,475	$11,475	$11,475	$11,475	$137,700	11.22%
$0	$0	$0	$0	$0	$0	$0	0.00%
$102,270	$102,270	$102,270	$102,270	$102,270	$102,270	$1,227,240	100%
$22,699	$22,699	$22,699	$22,699	$22,699	$22,699	$272,385	21.98%
$2,639	$2,639	$2,639	$2,639	$2,639	$2,639	$31,671	2.58%
$0	$0	$0	$0	$0	$0	$0	0.00%
$25,338	$25,338	$25,338	$25,338	$25,338	$25,338	$304,056	24.78%
24.78%	24.78%	24.78%	24.78%	24.78%	24.78%	24.78%	
$76,932	$76,932	$76,932	$76,932	$76,932	$76,932	$923,184	75.22%
75.22%	75.22%	75.22%	75.22%	75.22%	75.22%	75.22%	
$55,264	$55,251	$55,237	$55,223	$55,210	$55,196	$663,240	54.04%
$2,619	$2,619	$2,619	$2,619	$2,619	$2,619	$31,428	2.56%
$57,883	$57,870	$57,856	$57,842	$57,829	$57,815	$694,668	56.60%
56.60%	56.59%	56.57%	56.56%	56.55%	56.53%	56.60%	
$83,221	$83,208	$83,194	$83,180	$83,167	$83,153	$998,724	81.38%
81.37%	81.36%	81.35%	81.33%	81.32%	81.31%	81.38%	
$19,049	$19,062	$19,076	$19,090	$19,103	$19,117	$228,516	18.62%
18.63%	18.64%	18.65%	18.67%	18.68%	18.69%	18.62%	
$6,858	$6,863	$6,867	$6,872	$6,877	$6,883	$82,266	6.70%
6.71%	6.71%	6.71%	6.72%	6.72%	6.73%	6.70%	
$12,191	$12,199	$12,209	$12,218	$12,226	$12,234	$146,250	11.92%
11.92%	11.93%	11.94%	11.95%	11.95%	11.96%	11.92%	

Cash Flow Summary Years 1–5
The Oasis

For the year ending	Jul-05	Jul-06	Jul-07	Jul-08	Jul-09
Cash From Operations					
Food Revenues	$629,280	$786,600	$943,920	$1,089,540	$1,089,540
Beverage Revenues	$233,280	$108,000	$129,600	$137,700	$137,700
Merchandise Revenues	$0	$0	$0	$0	$0
Total Revenues	$862,560	$894,600	$1,073,520	$1,227,240	$1,227,240
Cash Available from Financing		$0	$0	$0	$0
Sale of Stock/Owner's Investment	$250,000	$0	$0	$0	$0
Mortgage	$0	$0	$0	$0	$0
Change in Accounts Payable	$66,107	$21,248	$9,568	$8,632	($23,181)
Long-Term Loan Proceeds	$90,000	$0	$0	$0	$0
Short-Term Loan Proceeds	$0	$0	$0	$0	$0
Sale of Investments	$0	$0	$0	$0	$0
Sale of Other Current Assets	$0	$0	$0	$0	$0
Sale of Other Assets	$0	$0	$0	$0	$0
Cash Available From Financing	$406,107	$21,248	$9,568	$8,632	($23,181)
Total Cash Available	$1,268,667	$915,848	$1,083,088	$1,235,872	$1,204,059
Cash Disbursements					
Cost of Goods Sold					

Cash Flow Summary Years 1–5 (continued)
The Oasis

For the year ending	Jul-05	Jul-06	Jul-07	Jul-08	Jul-09
Food	$157,320	$196,650	$235,980	$272,385	$272,385
Beverage	$53,654	$24,840	$29,808	$31,671	$31,671
Merchandise	$0	$0	$0	$0	$0
Total Cost of Goods Sold	$210,974	$221,490	$265,788	$304,056	$304,056
Accounting/Payroll Processing	$6,000	$6,300	$6,615	$6,946	$7,293
Administrative Salaries	$82,992	$82,992	$82,992	$82,992	$82,992
Admin Office Expenses	$6,000	$6,300	$6,615	$6,946	$7,293
Advertising & Promotions	$59,232	$62,194	$65,303	$68,568	$71,997
Bank Fees	$1,200	$1,260	$1,323	$1,389	$1,459
Credit Card Expense	$12,507	$12,972	$15,566	$17,795	$17,795
Insurance/Fire/Theft/ Liability/Liquor/Product	$30,000	$31,500	$33,075	$34,729	$36,465
Exterminator	$2,400	$2,520	$2,646	$2,778	$2,917
Legal Fees	$2,400	$2,520	$2,646	$2,778	$2,917
Licenses and Permits	$2,400	$2,520	$2,646	$2,778	$2,917
Royalty Fees	$0	$0	$0	$0	$0
Payroll Staff	$198,482	$208,406	$218,826	$229,768	$241,256
Professional Fees/Other	$2,400	$2,520	$2,646	$2,778	$2,917
Paper Supplies	$18,000	$18,000	$19,845	$20,837	$21,879
Lease Payment	$24,000	$25,200	$26,460	$27,783	$29,172
Repairs and Maintenance	$12,000	$12,600	$13,230	$13,892	$14,586
Trash Removal	$18,000	$18,900	$19,845	$20,837	$21,879
Real Estate Taxes (CEMC)	$0	$0	$0	$0	$0
Taxes Payroll/FICA	$21,533	$22,292	$23,089	$23,926	$24,805
Taxes Payroll/FUTA	$2,815	$2,914	$3,018	$3,128	$3,242

Cash Flow Summary Years 1–5 (continued)
The Oasis

For the year ending	Jul-05	Jul-06	Jul-07	Jul-08	Jul-09
Taxes Payroll/SUTA	$5,629	$5,828	$6,036	$6,255	$6,485
Telephone	$9,600	$10,080	$10,584	$11,113	$11,669
Utilities	$24,000	$25,200	$26,460	$27,783	$29,172
Workers' Compensation	$18,296	$18,941	$19,618	$20,329	$21,076
Total Operating Expenses	$559,886	$582,858	$609,085	$636,129	$662,185
Other Applications of Cash					
Land	$0	$0	$0	$0	$0
Buildings	$0	$0	$0	$0	$0
Leasehold Improvements	$16,750	$0	$0	$0	$0
Restaurant Equipment	$75,000	$0	$0	$0	$0
Furniture	$8,250	$0	$0	$0	$0
Delivery Van/Automobile	$0	$0	$0	$0	$0
Change in Inventory	$1,734	$86	$365	$314	$0
Purchase of Other Current Assets	$8,525	$0	$0	$0	$0
Purchase of Other Assets	$0	$0	$0	$0	$0
Purchase of Investments	$0	$0	$0	$0	$0
Dividends Payable	$0	$0	$0	$0	$0
Total Other Applications	$110,259	$86	$365	$314	$0
		$0	$0	$0	$0
Total Cash-Outlay	$881,119	$804,434	$875,238	$940,499	$966,241
Beginning Month Cash Balance	$250,000	$600,346	$674,580	$801,459	$983,427

Cash Flow Summary Years 1-5 (continued)
The Oasis

For the year ending	Jul-05	Jul-06	Jul-07	Jul-08	Jul-09
Ending Month Cash Balance	$637,548	$711,760	$882,430	$1,096,832	$1,221,245
Principal and Interest Payments					
Monthly Long-Term Debt Payment	$22,419	$22,419	$22,419	$22,419	$22,419
Monthly Mortgage Payment	$0	$0	$0	$0	$0
Total Principal and Interest Payments	$22,419	$22,419	$22,419	$22,419	$22,419
Beginning Month Cash Balance	$250,000	$600,346	$674,580	$801,459	$983,427
Ending Month Cash Balance	$615,124	$689,344	$860,015	$1,074,413	$1,198,830
Income Taxes	$14,778	$14,764	$58,556	$90,986	$82,266
Ending Year Cash Balance After Taxes	$600,346	$674,580	$801,459	$983,427	$1,116,564

Operating Budget Summary Years 1–5
The Oasis

For the year ending	Jul-05	Jul-06	Jul-07	Jul-08	Jul-09
Sales					
Food	$629,280	$786,600	$943,920	$1,089,540	$1,089,540
Beverage	$233,280	$108,000	$129,600	$137,700	$137,700
Merchandise	$0	$0	$0	$0	$0
Total Sales	$862,560	$894,600	$1,073,520	$1,227,240	$1,227,240
		4%	20%	14%	0%
Cost of Sales					
Food	$157,320	$196,650	$235,980	$272,385	$272,385
Beverage	$53,654	$24,840	$29,808	$31,671	$31,671
Merchandise	$0	$0	$0	$0	$0
Total Cost of Sales	$210,974	$221,490	$265,788	$304,056	$304,056
% of Total Sales	24.46%	24.46%	24.46%	24.78%	24.78%
Gross Profit	$651,586	$673,110	$807,732	$923,184	$923,184
% of Total Sales	75.54%	75.24%	75.24%	75.22%	75.22%
Operating Expenses					
Accounting/Payroll Processing	$6,000	$6,300	$6,615	$6,946	$7,293
Administrative Salaries	$82,992	$82,992	$82,992	$82,992	$82,992
Admin Office Expenses	$6,000	$6,300	$6,615	$6,946	$7,293
Advertising & Promotions	$59,232	$62,194	$65,303	$68,568	$71,997
Bank Fees	$1,200	$1,260	$1,323	$1,389	$1,459
Credit Card Expense	$12,507	$12,972	$15,566	$17,795	$17,795
Loan Interest Expense	$7,494	$6,094	$4,563	$2,888	$1,056
Principal Loan Payment	$14,925	$16,325	$17,856	$2,888	$21,204
Insurance/Fire/Theft/Liability/Liquor/Product	$30,000	$31,500	$33,075	$34,729	$36,465

Operating Budget Summary Years 1-5 (continued)
The Oasis

For the year ending	Jul-05	Jul-06	Jul-07	Jul-08	Jul-09
Exterminator	$2,400	$2,520	$2,646	$2,778	$2,917
Legal Fees	$2,400	$2,520	$2,646	$2,778	$2,917
Licenses and Permits	$2,400	$2,520	$2,646	$2,778	$2,917
Royalty Fees	$0	$0	$0	$0	$0
Payroll Staff	$198,482	$208,406	$218,826	$229,768	$241,256
Professional Fees/Other	$2,400	$2,520	$2,646	$2,778	$2,917
Paper Supplies	$18,000	$18,000	$19,845	$20,837	$21,879
Lease Payment	$24,000	$25,200	$26,460	$27,783	$29,172
Repairs and Maintenance	$12,000	$12,600	$13,230	$13,892	$14,586
Trash Removal	$18,000	$18,900	$19,845	$20,837	$21,879
Real Estate Taxes (CEMC)	$0	$0	$0	$0	$0
Taxes Payroll/FICA	$21,533	$22,292	$23,089	$23,926	$24,805
Taxes Payroll/FUTA	$2,815	$2,914	$3,018	$3,128	$3,242
Taxes Payroll/SUTA	$5,629	$5,828	$6,036	$6,255	$6,485
Telephone	$9,600	$10,080	$10,584	$11,113	$11,669
Utilities	$24,000	$25,200	$26,460	$27,783	$29,172
Workers' Compensation	$18,296	$18,941	$19,618	$20,329	$21,076
Total Operating Expenses	$559,886	$582,858	$609,085	$636,129	$662,185
% of Total Sales	67.51%	67.66%	58.83%	52.30%	55.77%
Total Expenses	$793,279	$826,767	$897,293	$945,961	$988,501
% of Total Sales	92.42%	83.58%	77.08%	80.55%	
Net Profit Before Income Taxes	$69,281	$67,833	$176,227	$281,279	$238,739
% of Total Sales	8.03%	7.58%	16.42%	22.92%	19.45%

Operating Budget Summary Years 1–5 (continued)
The Oasis

For the year ending	Jul-05	Jul-06	Jul-07	Jul-08	Jul-09
Taxes on Income	$19,399	$18,993	$63,442	$109,699	$85,946
% of Total Sales	2.25%	2.12%	5.91%	8.94%	7.00%
Net Income After Taxes	$49,882	$48,840	$112,785	$171,580	$152,793
% of Total Sales	5.78%	5.46%	10.51%	13.98%	12.45%

Income Statements Summary Years 1–5
The Oasis

For the year ending	Jul-05	Jul-06	Jul-07	Jul-08	Jul-09
Sales					
Food	$629,280	$786,600	$943,920	$1,089,540	$1,089,540
Beverage	$233,280	$108,000	$129,600	$137,700	$137,700
Merchandise	$0	$0	$0	$0	$0
Total Sales	$862,560	$894,600	$1,073,520	$1,227,240	$1,227,240
		4%	20%	14%	0%
Cost of Sales					
Food	$157,320	$196,650	$235,980	$272,385	$272,385
Beverage	$53,654	$24,840	$29,808	$31,671	$31,671
Merchandise	$0	$0	$0	$0	$0
Total Cost of Sales	$210,974	$221,490	$265,788	$304,056	$304,056
% of Total Sales	24.46%	24.46%	24.46%	24.78%	24.78%
Gross Profit	$651,586	$673,110	$807,732	$923,184	$923,184
% of Total Sales	75.54%	75.24%	75.24%	75.22%	75.22%

Income Statements Summary Years 1–5 (continued)
The Oasis

For the year ending	Jul-05	Jul-06	Jul-07	Jul-08	Jul-09
Gross Profit	$651,586	$673,110	$807,732	$923,184	$923,184
% of Total Sales	75.54%	75.24%	75.24%	75.22%	75.22%
Operating Expenses					
Operating Expenses (without Depreciation)	$567,380	$588,952	$613,648	$639,017	$663,240
Depreciation	$31,428	$31,428	$31,428	$31,428	$31,428
Total Operating Expenses	$598,808	$620,380	$645,076	$670,445	$694,668
% of Total Sales	69.42%	69.35%	60.09%	54.63%	56.60%
Total Expenses	$809,783	$841,870	$910,864	$974,501	$998,724
% of Total Sales	93.88%	94.11%	84.85%	79.41%	81.38%
Income From Operations	$52,777	$52,730	$162,656	$252,739	$228,516
% of Total Sales	6.12%	5.89%	15.15%	20.59%	18.62%
Taxes on Income	$14,778	$14,764	$58,556	$90,986	$82,266
% of Total Sales	1.71%	1.65%	5.45%	7.41%	6.70%
Net Income After Taxes	$37,999	$37,966	$104,100	$161,753	$146,250
% of Total Sales	4.41%	4.24%	9.70%	13.18%	11.92%
EBITDA	$91,700	$90,252	$198,647	$287,055	$260,999
% of Total Sales	10.63%	10.09%	18.50%	23.39%	21.27%

Balance Sheets Summary Years 1–5
The Oasis

For the year ending	Jul-05	Jul-06	Jul-07	Jul-08	Jul-09
Assets					
Current Assets					
Cash	$615,124	$689,344	$860,015	$1,074,413	$1,198,830
Investments	$0	$0	$0	$0	$0
Inventory	$1,734	$1,820	$2,185	$2,499	$2,499
Other Current Assets	$8,525	$8,525	$8,525	$8,525	$8,525
Total Current Assets	$625,383	$699,689	$870,725	$1,085,437	$1,209,854
Fixed Assets					
Land	$0	$0	$0	$0	$0
Buildings	$0	$0	$0	$0	$0
Building/Leasehold Improvements	$16,750	$16,750	$16,750	$16,750	$16,750
Restaurant Equipment	$155,000	$155,000	$155,000	$155,000	$155,000
Furniture	$48,250	$48,250	$48,250	$48,250	$48,250
Delivery Van/Automobiles	$0	$0	$0	$0	$0
Goodwill	$0	$0	$0	$0	$0
Less Accumulated Depreciation	($31,428)	($62,856)	($94,284)	($125,712)	($157,140)
Total Fixed Assets	$188,572	$157,144	$125,716	$94,288	$62,860
Other Assets	$0	$0	$0	$0	$0
Total Assets	$813,955	$856,833	$996,441	$1,179,725	$1,272,714

Balance Sheets Summary Years 1–5 (continued)
The Oasis

For the year ending	Jul-05	Jul-06	Jul-07	Jul-08	Jul-09
Liabilities					
Current Liabilities					
Short-Term Debt	$24,568	$24,568	$24,568	$24,568	$24,568
Accounts Payable	$66,107	$87,355	$96,923	$105,555	$82,374
Notes Payable/Mortgage	$0	$0	$0	$0	$0
Other Payables	$5,000	$5,000	$5,000	$5,000	$5,000
Accrued Liabilities	$0	$0	$0	$0	$0
Total Current Liabilities	$95,675	$116,923	$126,491	$135,123	$87,374
Long-Term Debt	$75,075	$58,751	$40,894	$21,363	$0
Total Liabilities	$170,750	$175,674	$167,385	$156,486	$87,374
Owner's Equity/ Stockholder					
Owner's Equity Common Stock	$250,000	$250,000	$250,000	$250,000	$250,000
Retained Earnings	$34,797	$72,765	$179,358	$331,702	$479,240
Earnings Distributed/ Dividends Paid	$0	$0	$0	$0	$0
Total Owner's Equity	$288,001	$325,969	$433,471	$595,224	$741,474
Total Liabilities & Equity	$813,955	$856,833	$996,441	$1,179,725	$1,272,714

Prepare For Success

Learn How to Be Profitable

Act, Not React

Navigate Pitfalls

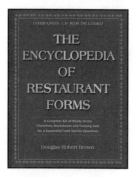
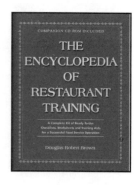
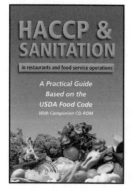

1-800-541-1336 Call toll-free
24 hours a day, 7 days a week.
Or fax completed form to:
1-352-622-5836 Order online!
Just go to www.atlantic-pub.com for
fast, easy, secure ordering.

Qty	Order Code	Book Title	Price	Total
	Item # RMH-02	THE RESTAURANT MANAGER'S HANDBOOK	$79.95	
	Item # FS1-01	Restaurant Site Location	$19.95	
	Item # FS2-01	Buying & Selling A Restaurant Business	$19.95	
	Item # FS3-01	Restaurant Marketing & Advertising	$19.95	
	Item # FS4-01	Restaurant Promotion & Publicity	$19.95	
	Item # FS5-01	Controlling Operating Costs	$19.95	
	Item # FS6-01	Controlling Food Costs	$19.95	
	Item # FS7-01	Controlling Labor Costs	$19.95	
	Item # FS8-01	Controlling Liquor, Wine & Beverage Costs	$19.95	
	Item # FS9-01	Building Restaurant Profits	$19.95	
	Item # FS10-01	Waiter & Waitress Training	$19.95	
	Item # FS11-01	Bar & Beverage Operation	$19.95	
	Item # FS12-01	Successful Catering	$19.95	
	Item # FS13-01	Food Service Menus	$19.95	
	Item # FS14-01	Restaurant Design	$19.95	
	Item # FS15-01	Increasing Restaurant Sales	$19.95	
	Item # FSALL-01	Entire 15-Book Series	$199.95	

➤ Best Deal! SAVE 33%
All 15 books for $199.95

Subtotal	
Shipping & Handling	
Florida 6% Sales Tax	
TOTAL	

SHIP TO:

Name_____Phone(____) _____

Company Name _____

Mailing Address _____

City _____State _____Zip _____

FAX _____E-mail _____

☐ My check or money order is enclosed   ☐ Please send my order COD   ☐My authorized purchase order is attached

☐ Please charge my: ☐ Mastercard ☐ VISA   ☐ American Express   ☐ Discover

Card # ☐☐☐☐-☐☐☐☐-☐☐☐☐-☐☐☐☐   Expires ☐☐☐☐

Please make checks payable to:
Atlantic Publishing Company • 1210 SW 23rd Place • Ocala, FL 34474-7014
USPS Shipping/Handling: add $5.00 first item, and $2.50 each additional or $15.00 for the whole
set. Florida residents PLEASE add the appropriate sales tax for your county.